"Angela Dee takes us on a journey of love, loss, heartbreak and triumph. Seen through the eyes and told through the words only a mother would know. A must read for a family with a special needs child."

-**Leslie Gustafson**, LMFT
– Sex and Psychotherapist
-Author of *Amazing Intimacy*,
Fox Denver's Sex and Marriage Therapist
AuthenticandTrue.com

"Spencer's illness forever changed the life of he and his family. They picked up the pieces and moved forward. As I read this book, I understood to a greater level the bond between mother and son. The love they share reminds me of God's grace in life's difficult circumstances.

Voiceless teaches us to never, never give up. Spencer's warrior-like spirit touches a depth far beyond our understanding. A true child of God, this is a must read for families with a special needs child or those facing life's difficult struggles. Highly recommend!"

-**J.R. Polhemus**,
Head Pastor,
The Rock Church, therock.org

"*Voiceless* tells the story of the power of non-verbal communication. Spencer's life is a great reminder that words don't always tell the story. A compelling read."

-**Carrie Escalante**,
Area Director
bethesdalutherancommunities.org

D1413163

"So many special needs families feel alone and isolated. Through the pages of *Voiceless* you will not only find that you are not alone, but I believe that you will also find a friend. In this book, Angela shines a light for many walking down a dark and unknown road. Both brave in their own way, Angela and Spencer encourage all of us to live anything but ordinary. Expect to be changed as you read *Voiceless*.

-**Celeste Barnard**,
Writer, Speaker, and Storyteller
-Celestebarnard.com

"We go to the movie theater to lose ourselves in some inspiring story about a make-believe super hero who is fighting a battle to save the world or rescue someone. These movies are made purposely to leave us feeling brave, even optimistic, like we could conquer the world. All because the actor defeated evil and made all the wrong things right. *Voiceless*-Spencer's Story, is a book about a *real life* super-hero, Spencer's Mom. Only in reality, life isn't always easily conquered. It almost never finishes its story with everything tied up neat and pretty with a bow on top. *Voiceless* is a true story about super heroes and battles, painful choices and relentless hope.

Within these pages you will feel a frightened mother's frustrations, heartbreaks, and deepest fears. But you will also be inspired and encouraged to determinedly persevere in the face of life's challenging obstacles. Most of all, you will hear *The Voice* of unconditional, never ending love-loud and clear."

-**Karla Swanigan**,
Minister and Speaker KarlaSwanigan.com

VOICELESS

Reverend Linda ~
Be Brave ~
Dream Big ~

Angela Dee ♡

Hebrews 11:1

VOICELESS

SPENCER'S STORY

A MOTHER'S JOURNEY RAISING A SON WITH SIGNIFICANT NEEDS

ANGELA DEE

Published by Author Academy Elite
P.O. Box 43, Powell, OH 43035
www.AuthorAcademyElite.com

ISBN: 978-1-943526-74-1
ISBN: 978-1-943526-73-4

Library of Congress Control Number: 2016912929
Author Academy Elite, Powell, OH

This book is dedicated to my Sweet Spencer Lee.
No other soul on earth has taught me so much about how to truly **live**.

My mission in life is not merely to *survive*, but to *thrive*; and to do so with *passion*, some *compassion*, some *humor*, and some *style*.
Dr. Maya Angelou

Igniting Souls Tribe,
Being influenced by Souls on Fire pushed me to the finish line. Thank-you.

Contents

Foreword

Angela Dee's journey with her son Spencer touched me in a way very few stories ever have.

I was interviewing candidates for Author Academy Elite one Saturday. Angela had seven minutes to convince me their story was one that needed to be told.

I immediately heard in her voice a mother who had weathered a long and devastating storm. The winds and tide had carried her into a new reality.

It's been said that a parent should never have to lose a child. But in a period of two short weeks, Angela lost her ornery, active six-year-old boy to the severe effects of viral encephalitis. Losing a child to brain injury then picking up the pieces and moving into a new status quo is life changing, to say the least. But that is exactly what Angela, Russ and her family did.

As she told me about Spencer, I came to understand that the bond between a mother and son is special indeed. Those who are closest to Spencer have found his unique ability to communicate through his eyes. They can silently hear his *thank you* and *I love you*. I knew it would be a one-of-a-kind story that others needed to hear. A mighty warrior within, Spencer's spirit and deep spiritual relationship with God reaches to a depth only he can understand.

Voiceless-Spencer's Story brings us through trauma, tragedy, and the five stages of grief. While the family settles into a new reality of raising a son with significant needs, Angela speaks raw truth about real life situations. The family shows us why unconditional love and following the passions of your heart brings healing.

This book that you are holding in your hands has emerged through 16 years of living with a speechless child who has changed each person that has been close enough to listen. Prepare to be challenged and learn as you read *Voiceless*. And maybe, like me, you will be changed in the process.

"Those who have a voice must speak for the Voiceless."

Kary Oberbrunner
CEO of Redeem the Day and Igniting Souls. Co-creator of Author Academy Elite.

Author of *Day Job to Dream Job, The Deeper Path, and Your Secret Name* and *ELIXIR Project*

Author's Note

Spencer's Story is written from my point of view. Over the last 16 years, MANY people have been involved in our lives. We are grateful for each individual as you were an important part of the journey. Spencer's everyday heroes have his/her own version of this story. After the book is released, I am excited to hear them.

There is another book on the horizon—a culmination of how Spencer has affected the lives of others. I will be collecting stories. If you have one, please send it to authorangeladee@gmail.com. You can also check out my website at angeladee.life.

Some of the names of the people mentioned in this book have been changed. I have done so where I felt anonymity was necessary.

PART I

THE CALM BEFORE
THE STORM

"Life was good. Everything was going right. It was almost scaring her because usually when things were going well it was the calm before the storm hit."

Michelle Sutton

1

A Dream Fulfilled

February 2000

To me, the ocean spills out all the great mysteries of life as it reaches the shore. It is complicated, compelling, and all consuming as much as it is graceful and calming. It is overly frightening, equally intriguing—and *always* powerful. You can watch the ocean all day long; you can stare at it into the night. The strength that lies beneath its surface is limitless, like one's own internal world. "Our fear is not that we are inadequate," said Marianne Williamson, "Our fear is that we are powerful beyond measure." My thoughts ride on the rolling sapphire blue sea. The white-tipped waves and the calming drum of the tide relax me. The cool, yet sun-kissed breeze refreshes my face with a fine salt mist and I lick my lips to taste it; to taste life. This reassures me that yes, we are *finally* on vacation. Ahhhh! Hurrah for a week with no worries!

Before me are the four loves of my life. Russ, my husband, and our three children, Evan, Spencer, and Elle–all perfect in God's image, and perfect in mine. Their silhouettes are dancing against the setting sun, happy, carefree, and loving life. The sunset is simply gorgeous with hues of red, orange, and yellow streaking the sky. The outer edge pulsates and resembles a ball of fire.

Our Elle is now two and is overwhelmed by the massiveness of the ocean, seeing it for the first time. Safe in Daddy's arms, she is shaking her hands up and down, squealing with delight.

Evan, now eight, inches his way into the surf, wanting to be fully immersed in the coolness of the water. I visualize him with his bleached blonde hair and slender body diving and snorkeling and wading through tide pools. We remind him of the powerful undertow and he runs to join Spencer. Though they have quite different personalities they balance one another. Could they be best buddies for life?

Our five-year-old Spencer is chasing the tide as it goes out, yelling, "Nana nana nana, can't catch me!" He turns around and giggles with excitement as the waves chase him back to the beach and his toes have a wet layer of sand covering them. He screams and runs faster, just before the water has a chance to tag his heels. At this moment, Spencer resembles the setting sun. His shyness dissolves as the power of the ocean reveals his competitive nature and love of life. In only months, he will be headed into the vastness of the unknown. Instead of running out of the ocean, he will sink down into it.

But for now, my childhood vision of being a mother and wife is fulfilled. My family is complete and my dream a reality.

2

Spencer's Birth Story

June 3, 1994

With all three of my young-
sters, Evan, Spencer, and
Elle, I started a journal of
their development in the
early years of life. From birth
to five years, I wrote of their
funny goings-on, cute say-
ings, illnesses, and milestones
attained. I penned in a few
stories that are often relayed
to us through parents or relatives when we are old enough
to care.

     With the birth of my second son, Spencer, my pregnancy
seemed quite different from the first. I didn't experience
morning sickness and wasn't constantly hungry. Certain I
was having a girl we had only had girls' names picked out.

     While at the grocery store check-out, the elderly woman
in front of me reached out to rub my belly and asked, "When
are you due dear?"

"June 1st," I said.

"Are you having a boy or girl?" she asked.

"This one's going to surprise me!"

After three false labors, many walks around the park, the start of contractions, followed by more contractions and even more contractions . . . we still did not have a baby to show for my hard labors. The contractions would suddenly stop and start up just as we left the hospital again and then again. "Dysfunctional contractions" is what the doctor was calling it and he attempted to induce labor followed by broken water. No baby. Then there was the introduction of Pitocin to speed up delivery, and an epidural, and . . . voila . . . Spencer was born 24 hours later. FINALLY. Hallelujah!

On June 3, 1994 at 6:45 pm our new baby boy entered this world screaming. He was healthy, strong, and looked just like daddy . . . but he needed a name. Dr. Carl called out, "A new baby boy, what will his name be?"

"Austin or Jesse or Spencer Lee…we're not sure," Proud poppa Russ quipped.

Dad cut the umbilical cord, laid Spencer on my belly and he stopped crying instantly. I welcomed another perfect little boy into our lives. I smiled thinking Evan would now have a playmate and best friend in his new baby brother. The joy overtook me, just as powerful as the first time, and I cried at such a wonderful miracle. *Thank you, God.*

A few hours later we decided on a name as we were remembering a conversation Russ had had with his father, Greg, a couple days before. Greg was at our house visiting during my labor "walkabout" period and jokingly said, "If she is not careful, she is going to have that baby on Spencer Street."

Russ and his dad shared a chuckle and I just rolled my eyes, "Yeah, right. That's not gonna happen."

Since *we* lived on Spencer Street that was the joke and, consequently, that's how Spencer got his name. Spencer Lee McCombs. Spencer means dispenser of provisions, one who supplies and provides something for others. And Lee was chosen for my paternal grandfather's name, meaning meadow.

'Twas The Night Before Spencer
Christmas Letter 1994

'Twas the night before Spencer and all through the house,
Only Angie was stirring, busy stuffing her mouth.
The bags were all packed in the crib where they lay,
In hopes our new bundle would soon find his way.
With Evan and Russ snug in their beds,
Angie was in labor with a rag on her head.
Russ called from bed with Ang on the couch,
Trying to sleep, she repeated the word, O-U-C-H.
When pains became stronger and Angie grew fatter,
Russ was always there to help in the matter.
On the eve of June 2nd through the pouring rain,
We decided to GO, Angie moaning in pain.
Just when we thought Angie might suddenly pop,
We finally arrived only to have her labor stop.
When what to our wondering eyes should appear,
But a room full of nurses all saying, "Stay here."
With very little sleep and inducement for labor,
Angie knew in a moment she'd be asking for favors.
As slowly as an inchworm our little miracle came,
They shouted "it's a boy" and called out for a name.
"Is it Spencer or Austin or Jesse or Lee?"

"Which one have you chosen, what will his name be?"
"Spencer Lee," said his father, "another boy in the clan."
What a fine healthy baby, all part of God's plan.
Then he drew his first breath and that loud cry rang out.
He looks just like Russ, of that there's no doubt.
Evan was with grandma being spoiled to the core.
They came to the hospital and peeked through the door.
He was excited and happy upon entering the room.
A little apprehension, when it hit with a boom.
"Evan come see your brother, he's got your cute nose."
His interest was in his new fire truck with the long water hose.
"No! I want *my* cute nose," Evan said with conviction.
We could tell at that moment, it was the start of some friction.
Things ran quite smoothly for a short little while
Then jealousy crept in taking over Ev's smile.
While baby was sleeping and mom was in the shower,
It was Evan's chance to show who had power.
With scissors in hand, Evan went straight to his work
Snip snipping away at Spencer's blue shirt.
This was only one of many instances you know,
And once little brother got bit on the toe.
The adjustment's been hard but life is much funner;
Ev talks about playing with Spencer next summer.
So…we exclaim to all parents entering parenthood twice,
Learn lots of patience; calm down and be nice.

3

Normal Years

1994-2000

At seven days old, I took Spencer back to the doctor for his circumcision. Post-partum craziness was in full swing and I sat in the waiting area with tears streaming down my face. Spencer was wailing at the top of his lungs in the room  next door. It was the first time I felt a tug on my heartstrings for this child. We made a fine pair no matter how far apart we were.

"I think that is the strongest, stubborn newborn I have ever seen! He fought me hard the entire time; a mighty warrior. Here you go momma. Good luck with *this* one," the doctor said as he eagerly handed me a tightly swaddled, whimpering Spencer.

As a baby Spencer was easy going. He ate well, slept through the night after two weeks and was happy most of the time. This boy had a temper when he got mad and it was then that we knew the power of his strength. If he was awake the "on" switch did not turn off until he hit the pillow. Even then, it took him awhile to fall asleep. He didn't like to sleep; he was afraid he would miss something. Spencer liked being held facing forward so he could look the world straight on and kick, smile, and scream at it with all that he had.

Wrestling and tickling with Dad and Evan were among his favorite things to do. After pulling himself up to a standing position at six months, he was determined to clear the shelves, pull dirt out of plants, and destroy whatever he could and as fast as he could. This became a little game between "Buggy" and me and he loved it. At ten months, when he was mostly upright and walking around furniture, I watched Spencer pull a hair off of Dad's shirt and then string it through his forefinger and thumb on the opposite hand. *Nice fine motor skills*, I thought. By eleven months we got out of *his* way as he was walking on his own. While his physical abilities soared, his speech took a little longer to acquire.

For that entire first year, Spencer was continuously on antibiotics for recurring ear infections. After both eardrums ruptured, the doctor explained that Spencer's Eustachian tubes sat at an angle where fluid could not easily drain. The tubes needed to evacuate so that the infections would stop. Spencer's speech picked up after surgery, and we wondered if he only heard muffled sounds before. With continued use of so many antibiotics we read that his immune system could be weakened and we did notice that Spencer was always the first in the family to get sick.

Spencer's first year was spent growing quickly and building memories with his brother. One spring morning, I walked out into the sunshine and felt grateful for the two healthy boys sitting in the sandbox playing with backhoes. Evan's little boy voice was explaining to Spencer how to lift the bucket with the lever on the side of the backhoe. With Spence, though, there was no need for demonstration from his older brother. He got it!

By the time Spencer was two, he was beating up his brother. If Spencer didn't get his way, he got physical. "Use your words," meant nothing to Spencer. Evan, a peacemaker, wanted to talk it through. As the older brother, he knew not to hit, so he would stand there and whimper trying to explain to Spencer why "we do not hit." Spencer had his sweet snuggly moments, but for the most part he was one rough and tumble kid. By the time the boys were four and six we had invented an activity called the "peace rug". Whenever there was a disagreement or fight, they had to sit back to back at opposite ends of the rug until they were ready to talk calmly. When I wasn't watching, Spencer would turn around and thwack Evan in the head, then turn back around and giggle. When they were able to sit face-to-face we practiced using words like, "Spencer it made me feel _____ when you did _____." Spencer never got it. It frustrated Evan, but then it usually turned into a giggle fest. Some days there was a lot of time spent on the rug.

One morning we found Spencer in the kitchen cupboard eating a mouthful of vitamins. When he was obsessed with keys, he would find a set and insist on trying to stick them into the electrical outlets. Inevitably, he'd find the one that didn't have a childproof cap in it. Or he'd pull out all the childproof covers and then play. One day he got a hold of some powdered cleanser and sprinkled it all over the bathroom floor. When I came to the door he said, "No fanking mommy, No fanking." Because Spencer heard some nightly call to explore the house, a safety gate was placed in his way.

When I was pregnant with Elle, he would walk up to me and hit my stomach, then giggle. When I scolded him, he'd gently lift up my shirt and kiss my tummy. Spencer earned plenty of time outs! And if I tried to talk to him while in his time-out he would say, "Don't talk to me, I'm in time-out." When I would call him "cutie" he'd say, "I'm not cutie; I'm Fencer."

Spencer loved music and dancing. He favored southern and classic rock, hip hop, and later classical music. The Beatles' White Album and Aerosmith were among his favorites. I Believe I Can Fly by R. Kelly was his favorite song. When he was about two, I would tuck him in at night and say his prayers. Afterward he would always look up at me with those beautiful brown eyes and ask, "Mommy, sing Sunshine Way." And so I would sing *You Are My Sunshine*. Then he would say, "Tinkle Tinkle?" And I would sing *Twinkle, Twinkle Little Star*.

"Tanks Mommy," he'd say.

"I love you Spencer."

"I wuv you too," and then he'd plead, "No fence Mommy. No fence."

As Spencer entered pre-school, he became a quick learner. He enjoyed science and recess, and was noticeably shy. He loved school. At home he was more competitive in riding bikes, rollerblading, basketball, or baseball. He was a *poor* loser and had to be taught how to lose gracefully. His solution: don't lose! One-on-one was his favorite activity with anyone who would take him on in *anything*. After much deliberating over war toys, Spencer got a light saber for his fourth birthday. He spent life in his Spiderman jammies and sports jerseys, sleeping soundly with his light saber and trading cards. His inner neat-nick put all his toys in a row. He'd get upset when his toddler sister would mess up the house. He'd say, "Mom I am not a destroyer anymore, Elle is." Spencer often helped fold laundry, clean toilets, or put groceries away. His favorite words at four were "actually" and "completely". And at the end of an especially good day he would say, "Mom I want to rewind this day."

At four, Spencer was inquisitive about death and dying. He asked, "Do you know how God made us? Where do you go when you die? Where's heaven? Where's God? Who was the first person in heaven? Am I, new or old? I don't want to die." Spencer's intriguing and unique relationship with God reached far deeper than what he'd been taught by us or by anyone at church. Many of the questions he asked, I could  not answer. Sometimes I would see him perfectly still, not engaging in anything.

I would ask, "What are you doing Spencer?"

"Praying in my mind," he'd say.

Out of the wild yonder he said, "Mom, if you die, I want another mom just like you. I love you, Mom." His questions were always met with a wrinkled brow. Sometimes I wondered if he could see things that we could not. One day I walked into the kitchen and heard him say, "I love you very much Jesus." Then he proceeded to sing to the cross around his neck. That same night we found him asleep on our bedroom floor. Around 10:30 p.m. I heard Spencer talking.

"Spencer, GO TO SLEEP," I demanded.

"I can't. Jesus is keeping me awake," he said.

"Oh, really. What's he doing?" I asked.

"He's talking to me," he said.

"Well, what is he saying?"

"He is telling the bad man to behave."

"I thought he was talking to *you*?" I inquired.

"I can hear them talking to each other," he said.

"Well if you want to continue talking to Jesus, could you please whisper?" Now I'm wide awake.

"Okay Mom, love you." He acted as if this were just another normal activity.

Another time, at the end of our nightly prayers, I asked if there was anyone else we needed to pray for. That night he was insistent on praying for his Uncle Shawn. "Okay, Spencer. Why don't you pray," I encouraged.

"Dear God, I know Uncle Shawn is really in trouble. I want you to keep him safe. Help him with whatever is bothering him. Thank you, Jesus."

And then my mother called to say my brother was struggling and would be home from school abroad within the week.

 During the summer, Spencer loved to hike, camp, and fish. When we hiked as a family, he was always out far ahead of us. I'd have to call him back when he got out of sight, so he usually hiked twice as far as the rest of us. One day on our way up the Castle Rock, he was ignited with conversation. I was glad he wanted to talk, because then I didn't have to try to catch up to *him*.

"Hey Mom, what things come from cows?"

"I don't know Spence, tell me."

"Cowlifornias. Haha, I made a joke."

"That's funny Spencer," piped Evan.

Then Evan stopped on the path to study a bug. Spencer ordered, "Let's move along, Evan. Come now."

We were hiking the trail up to Mesa Verde when Spencer turned and said, "Mom, I'm really glad God made me. I like myself. I'm glad God gave me you for a mom too."

"Thanks Spencer," I replied, swallowing the lump in my throat.

"Hey Mom, could you make me some real feathery wings so I can fly?"

"Oh sure honey . . . in my free time." *Nothing to it,* I thought, *with a 2, 5, and a 7 year old!*

The excursion to Mesa Verde was frustrating because the boys could not smash or climb on anything. They got tired of being told that there were too many artifacts and ancient ruins that could *not* be touched. I wondered if Spencer just wanted to fly over them instead. Then he could see but not have to touch.

About a month before he learned to tie his shoe, he had started asking me, "Would you be so kind as to tie my shoe?" His politeness was his way of showing me that he was getting tired of asking for favors and he knew I was tired of tying. Once Spencer set his mind to something, it was as good as done. So this mini problem was about to be solved just as soon as Spencer jumped on it.

The week that Spencer began kindergarten, he got his training wheels off his bike, rode the school bus for the first time, and lost his first tooth. Milestones! But he still had not conquered the art of tying his shoelaces and seemed determined to put this one under his belt. "Would you be so kind as to tie my shoe?" he asked. And then he would ask again. And again I would tie up his shoes. He would ask yet again, and I would strap him in. I found a box and punched holes in the lid, then laced the lid like a big shoe so that he could put it in his lap and practice. By the time we left for school at 11:30 Spencer had it mastered. Now *that's* tying one on!

| 16 |

4

My Alma Mater

April 20, 1999

"The definition of normal changed that day."
Columbine student

Our house sat up on a hill, overlooking our small budding town. On the horizon are the jagged edges of Colorado's Front Range. It was a warm day, sun glowing and a cool breeze teasing us with the scent of spring. Our three  children ran along the dirt road without a care, chasing the dog, kicking pebbles, and giggling with one another.

It was on this day we heard the news of the Columbine High School massacre. This horror story yanked us right out of our safe and secure suburban cocoon. Only 30 miles from home—and at my own high school no less—is the place where 12 students and 1 teacher were shot to death. The second safest place, next to home, wasn't safe anymore.

How do some souls transform from the innocence and wonder of children to young men who seem angry and confused? My heart was filling with fear because I realized I had no control over the situation, or really our kids for that matter. *Oh God, I don't understand why bad things happen to good people.* I asked God to surround the families and the victims with his protective strength and drench them in love. *I wish no one had to feel this pain. Father, bring the families of the victims closer to you. Don't allow the lies of darkness to enter their hearts. If something good can come from this tragedy, I pray that it would be used for your glory.* I took a deep breath and looked to the mountains. *Lord, I ask that you would ALWAYS protect my children, no matter where they go or what they do. Amen.*

The children were huddled around a patch of brown grass. Something had caught their attention. An Indian Paintbrush was coming into bloom and taunting a small butterfly that was admiring it, too. Reverently, I said, "Oh, kids, be still." As they eyed the butterfly with their steadfast wide gaze, the butterfly opened its wings and twitched at them to say hello. Their excitement moved its wings to flight. As we watched it flutter gracefully into the breeze, I knew my children would experience their own transformation and find their paths to greatness too.

PART II

THE EYE OF THE HURRICANE

"Do not judge. You don't know what storm I've asked them to walk through."

God

5

Summer Travels

June 1, 2000

We were taking a car trip to a family wedding and the rain was falling sideways. Surrounded, we could barely see in front of us and the tension in the van was rising. This weather, with a long day of travel, and the anticipation of getting to our destination was on everyone's mind. For a few moments all was quiet, except for the wind blowing and the rain beating on the car. I closed my eyes imagining that we were in a car wash.

"When you're sliding into first and your pants begin to burst, DIARRHEA, DIARRHEA!

When you're climbing up the ladder and your pants begin to splatter, DIARRHEA, DIARRHEA." Chimed Evan with Spencer, who were in the back seat singing in unison accented with giggles between. "It all seems kind of funny, but it's really brown and runny, DIARRHEA, DIARRHEA." My mom and I looked at each other and joined in their laughter.

"Mom, Spencer has to go to the bathroom," Evan said, giggling. "He thinks he's going to have DIARRHEA!" Spencer burst out laughing, but as he did, he let out a painful groan. My dad, our chauffeur, said, "This would be a good time to stop because I could use a break from the rain." We pulled in to the next gas station just outside of Wichita, Kansas. I helped Spencer into the bathroom and asked if he felt okay. He had a stomachache.

"Do you have a headache or sore throat, Bug?" I asked. I knew him well. He would never tell me when he was getting sick because he didn't want to miss out on anything. Usually he'd just get cranky, tired, or extra ornery.

"No, Mom. I just have to have diarrhea, that's all." That figures. I chalked it up to the candy and some junk food we had eaten in the car. Oh goodie, the joys of traveling.

We arrived at my aunt's house in Andale, Kansas, just in time to tuck our kiddos into bed. Tomorrow would be busy visiting with relatives and preparing for my cousin's wedding. It was good to be away from the constant decision-making we undertook for building our dream house on acreage in the country. Exciting as it was, it was also stressful. I was s-o-o-o-o glad for the brief getaway. I was missing Russ, who stayed behind to work. I felt a bit sorry that we would not be in our own home on Spencer's sixth birthday. We'd have to have an extra special celebration when we got home and hoped that his stomachache would get gone in a hurry!

6

Birthday Cake

June 2, 2000

It was a bright day in the small town of Andale. I wondered if I could manage a slower pace of life in this "don't blink" town, or if boredom would eventually set in. It felt like this little spot had a bubble around it, protecting it and isolating it from the rest of the world. Everything they needed was here. My cousin lived adjacent from the park and pool. Even his business was right in the neighborhood. The grocery store, church, and Grandma were all within walking distance of one another. The community was full of friends and family members, and everyone took care of one another. Why would one ever need to leave?

I found contentment in watching my children play on the merry-go-round. Sarah, my cousin's wife, and I were catching up since our last visit. Joyous screams of "stop!" erupted from the merry-go-round.

"Not too fast, Evan. You guys are going to get sick," I called out.

"It's okay, Mom. They *want* to go fast."

"When someone yells stop, you need to stop. Be careful when Elle is on. If you go too fast, she will slide off and get hurt."

"O-k-a-y, Mom." With the longest "a" possible! His tone was emphasizing each vowel as an indication that I was nagging. Sarah and I walked across the street to get a glass of iced tea. When we got back, Spencer was off of the merry-go-round and bent over by a tree. I walked over to see what was going on.

"Are you okay, Bug?" I asked.

"I need to throw up," he said.

"Too many turns on the merry-go-round, huh?" I rubbed his back as he purged, and I told him I was going to run to the car to get a wet wipe. I watched him as I went. He had his hands on his knees and his legs and arms were shaking. He continued to be sick. As I walked back, I noticed his chin moving back and forth. I assumed he was trying to get the icky off. When I tried to hand him the wipe, he did not respond. I bent down and pulled him up by his shoulders and looked into his eyes.

"You okay, Spence?" I asked tentatively. I looked him over again. His pupils were dilated and he seemed disoriented and worn. I shot over to tell Sarah something was wrong. When the two of us ran back, he was lying down on the grass, *asleep*!

"Buddy, you okay?"

"I just don't feel well. I need a nap," said the child who would never willingly rest. We laid him comfortably in the van and went on to Sarah's son's baseball game. Spencer slept through the entire thing.

When we got back to my aunt's house, Spencer woke up. He was lying on the couch, still not feeling well. He continued to have diarrhea but hadn't vomited anymore.

I sensed at that moment that he and I both knew he had something more than a flu bug.

"I don't want to be sick on my birthday," he moaned.

"Let's say a prayer, Bugaboo. *Lord, please help Spencer to feel better for his birthday. He wants to have fun and play. Thank-you Jesus. We love you.*

"Thanks Mom," he said. "Angie, do you want me to make a cake for Spencer's birthday tomorrow? It won't take any time at all," my aunt asked.

"Oh no, aunt Gigi. You don't need to do that. We have a nice party planned when we get home. We can have wedding cake for his birthday tomorrow. Thanks for offering," I said.

"You sure? It's no problem."

We had no idea that this would be Spencer's last opportunity to eat birthday cake.

7

Spencer's Sixth Birthday

June 3, 2000

The wedding was big and beautiful. My cousin, Marie, made a gorgeous bride and she and her handsome husband reminded me of wedding cake toppers . . . and, now, milestone makers. Spencer fell into his own kind of dream world during the ceremony while I smoothed his head and silently prayed that all would be well for everybody. We sat down to eat at the reception lunch, but all Spencer wanted was 7-Up. I told him that he could not get up to play until he had eaten at least half a plate of food. Afterward, I followed him to the restroom.

"How are you feeling buddy? Do you still have the squirts?"

"Yes, but I feel better than yesterday," he said. I reached down and felt his forehead. No fever.

"Let me know if you get worse or if you need anything, all right?"

"Okay, Mom," he replied. Then he ran off to find Evan.

The groom danced with his mother, and the bride with her father. Beautiful moments! Memories came to mind and moved me. I kept my eyes closed and previewed a future scene. I was the mother and Spencer the groom. He was all grown—so handsome and standing six inches taller than me. As we danced, I could hardly believe this was my Little Buggy all grown up. He was now a man, leaving his mother and father and preparing to make a home with his bride. The same vision came into my mind with Evan, and then of Russ dancing with Elle on *her* wedding day. In a flash I was jerked back to the moment, and suddenly needed to have a celebration dance with mister birthday boy. And right on cue, the DJ announced, "Hey, if any of you see a little boy named Spencer out there, tell him Happy Birthday. He is six years old today!"

I ran outside to find him playing among the dozens of cousins. With a lot of coaxing, he came in to dance with me. I picked him up and twirled him around in the air. "Come on Bug, it's your birthday. Let's go celebrate!" I placed him on my hip and hurried to the dance floor. With his face buried in my neck, we danced and twirled and tickled.

Everyone was wishing him happy birthday and patted his back, head, or shoulder, but he was trying to ignore it all. After two songs, he loosened up and hopped off my hip. His equally shy and quiet cousin, Erin, grabbed his hands. "Let's dance Spence. Come on!"

Looking down, Spencer shrugged his shoulders, put his finger up to his lip, and slightly turned his head, thinking. Slowly and gently, he took Erin's hands and began to dance. Because these two were alike, she was the perfect person to pull Spencer into the moment. A memory we would hold dear for years to come. We all took turns on the floor until everyone was tired and ready to call it a day. Spencer didn't look well.

I rationalized that he had to be feeling better since he had run around all day playing and with few complaints. My thoughts now could safely move on to other plans and how much time we would be here. Tomorrow we would go see my grandmother who was in a nursing home. She was 91 and in failing health. After having 15 children, who in turn gave her 79 grandchildren and countless great-grandchildren, I was amazed she was still living. After our visit, we would be leaving for Colorado.

As I drove home to my aunt's house, I went over the day's events, revisiting worry that I had only just settled. Was Spencer getting *better* or *worse*? He'd only picked at his cereal, but he didn't take much joy in breakfast, so there's nothing there. He was cheerful opening his birthday gifts, exactly as he should be. He strapped on his roller blades and skated up and down the sidewalk (with Elle following close behind on her tricycle) shrieking with excitement—all good. Despite these assurances, I could *feel* Spencer wasn't really himself.

At the table, Spencer turned to his brother and quietly said, "I love you, Evan." It's as if he knew he had to get it out and only loud enough for Evan to hear it. One of Spencer's last sentiments to his brother.

Evan smiled a little, and said, "I love you too, Spencer."

8

Amazing Helen

June 4, 2000

"Hello, Charlotte. Hello, Angela," my grandmother Helen said, as we walked into her room. "Who do we have here?" she asked, looking at Evan, Spencer, and Elle. At this stage in her life, she rarely remembered her grandchildren's names, let alone the great grandchildren. It hadn't always been this way. Only in the last five years had my grandmother's memory failed her. I was amazed by how she remembered all of us and could call us by name for decades on end.

One of the most precious things my grandmother did was to make birthday cards for her kids and grandkids. She had great artistic ability and was an aspiring writer. Each year I got a homemade birthday card created by Grandma's own buckled fingers ... right up until she moved to the nursing home. When I opened her cards, I would daydream about my grandmother sitting for hours at her kitchen table, sketching out and coloring the beautiful pictures, then choosing the one she made mine. These cards I kept in a keepsake chest that I got to honor her. When overcome with sweet thoughts of yesterdays or at times when I felt the world didn't appreciate me or I didn't appreciate myself, I would open this treasure chest. Grandma made each one of us feel special.

As I sat down to visit, I was in awe that my grandmother even remembered *my* name! After all, we lived out of state and visited infrequently and, were, naturally, the first faces she'd likely forget. It made sense. She had not called me by name for several years, but today she wasn't even coaxed. So we visited. I reminded her which of her children I belonged to (just in case) and we shared of our daily routines and anything left wanting in our hearts.

"Grandma, what have you used on your face all these years? Your skin is so beautiful!"

"Thank you, Angela. I just used Ponds Cold Cream, stayed out of the sun, and I always wore a hat."

Well, there you have it, I thought. The secret to younger looking skin: stay out of the sun and use a moisturizer full of mineral oil. No big bucks, Botox injections, or facelifts! Small town wisdom.

During Mother's visit with Grandma, I watched the kids in the courtyard chasing bunnies. Hopefully, they'll run off some energy and wind down to match the slower pace here. I noticed Spencer sitting on the bench, watching, as the other two siblings were trying to capture one of the bunnies. This was curious because he's usually the one leading the pack.

"You okay, buddy? You don't feel good, do you?"

"No," he said. The truth was he just felt so awful that he couldn't hide it anymore.

"Do you want to come in and sit on my lap for a while?" I asked.

"Yes," he said. So I rounded up his brother and sister and we came inside. We wrapped up our visit, gave Grandma lots of lovin' and I got to tell her again how much I respected and loved her. It was a feel-good reunion.

Back at my aunt's house, I called home to weave Russ back into our lives from afar. I shared about the wedding, and reported on Spencer's not-up–to-his-regular-self news. Russ settled me down and unknotted all the tension by his calm. We'll both see how Spencer was feeling in the morning and he should get over whatever it is soon anyway. He also mentioned how much he was accomplishing while we were gone. So with a little sweet talk from my aunt, we decided to stay for one more night. We'd start out fresh in the morning after a good night's rest.

9

Fear Defined

June 5, 2000

"Angie! Something is really wrong with Spencer," my dad said calmly, but the shadows lining his face gave him away. Spencer was chest-deep in the hotel hot tub. His body was stiff and shaking violently all over, robotically. His eyes rolled back in their sockets, and frothy saliva dripped down his chin. Panic! I jumped out of the pool, scooped Spencer tightly while I ran across the hall toward our room. I attempted to hold onto my slippery wet child and place the key card into its slot to open the door without him sliding onto the floor. *Breathe Angie,* I told myself, *breathe!* Spencer had a rapid pulse in his neck, thank God, but my heart was beating louder with terror. And then I looked him over as I set him on the bed. He was not breathing and his lips were turning purple.

Spencer began to vomit and I turned him over to avoid the muck aspirating into his lungs. I held the trash can up to his mouth and called 911. By now, Spencer was coming out of his seizure and belligerently trying to grab the trashcan out of my hands. Why was he angry? I was just happy to see him breathing again. I knew what to do during a seizure but then I also knew something was truly wrong to have one.

The paramedics and my dad walked into the room at the same time. They began to ask questions, check vital signs, and give Spencer oxygen. Still combative, Spencer tried to push the paramedics away. He did not like the fuss being made over him or around him. We tried to explain to him what had happened, but he was mad and confused. As they strapped him to the stretcher, the confusion turned to fear and he began to cry. I held his hand and assured him that these people were going to take good care of him and I would be close by. We were just going to the hospital to get things checked out. My dad offered to ride in the ambulance and do his best to keep Spencer calm. Grandma would stay with Evan and Elle. I told him I'd grab my clothes and follow them.

I ran to the van and quickly pulled out of the parking lot in pursuit of the ambulance. Lightning fear zigzagged its way through my veins while driving behind the steady pulse of the flashing red lights. No mother wants to be following an ambulance with her little boy in it. Tears blurred my vision and I quickly wiped them away.

Arriving at the hospital moments after they did, I ran through the double doors of Emergency when hospital guards appeared and tried to bar me from going in. "My little boy is in there," I said, and they let me pass. I could see the paramedics with the nurses wrestling to keep his wildly shaking body from flipping off the table. Spencer was having another seizure, more violent than the last.

"What is wrong with him? Can you tell me what's happening?" The doctor took me by the arm and tried to lead me out, explaining that he was having a seizure. He convinced me to slow myself down and come into a calmer environment so he could get more information.

"We *will* get to the bottom of this and find out why Spencer is having seizures. We found out in the ambulance that he is sensitive to Valium. The paramedics administered it to manage his seizure, but then he stopped breathing. They were about to intubate him when he started breathing on his own again. We will schedule at CAT scan, EEG, and spinal tap as soon as possible."

"Thank you," I said and paused, but not for long. "Would a head butt from a rollerblading accident a month ago have caused this? He wasn't wearing his helmet and he smacked it pretty good." The doctor promised he would check for bleeding in the brain.

"I see you are wearing a cross," the doctor said, changing the subject. "We have a chaplain who can come pray with you if you would you like me to call him."

"Oh, please," I pleaded. That would be nice, thank you." God gives grace when it is most needed, and I needed it right now.

The doctor said he'd send *them* over as he walked back into the ER. I wanted to follow him, but decided to change clothes so I wouldn't be in my swimsuit when the chaplain arrived.

I walked into the restroom and it was all I could do to get the door shut and locked before I fell to my knees and began to respond to my own delayed reactions. I cried and prayed. *Lord, PLEASE spare Spencer's life!* I heard my dad talking to someone in the waiting room. I hurried and got dressed… My dad introduced a middle-aged man and his son, both pastors at a local church. They asked me a few questions so they'd be able to offer the best prayer for the situation. We stood in a circle, strangers in this unfamiliar waiting room in small-town Kansas, holding hands and praying. Strangers or not, God was with us and it calmed me and gave me the strength I needed to get through the night.

10

No Signs

June 5, 2000

"Mommy, my head hurts," Spence moaned. He was lying in the next bed in Intensive Care at Memorial Hospital. "When can we go home? I don't like this place."

"Get some rest, Honey. I'll be right here all night. Your body has been through a lot. Next time the doctor comes in I'll ask if you can have something for the pain. If all goes well, which I'm sure it will, we can go home tomorrow," I said.

"Mom?"

"Yes, Honey?"

"Are we still going to have my birthday sleepover with my friends when we get home?"

"You bet. As soon as you feel better we'll bake a cake and plan a sleepover. Sound like a deal?"

"Yep. Good night. I love you Mom," he said, making sure that I wouldn't forget about his *real* party because we had been out of town. That and a gentle back rub was the lullaby he needed to fall into the Land of Nod.

Exhale, Angie, my inner voice chanted. And now . . . I *could* breathe. I called my mom to check in on Evan and Elle. They were fine, but mom had the flu. *The flu*. Could Spencer just have an aggravated flu bug? Hmm. Or maybe we should consider food poisoning too? We ate coming here and at the wedding, so let's put that on the list. I also called Russ to share the past hours of upsetting news. He offered to come out to Colby and ride home with us on the following day. Just then my eyes caught sight of the doctor and a nurse watching through the windows of their adjacent room.

"You'd better get some sleep while *he's* sleeping," the doctor suggested.

"Oh, I can't sleep right now. There are too many unanswered questions."

"You know this could be as simple as the beginning stages of epilepsy. When kids grow, they access different parts of their brain that haven't been used yet. They may tap into an area that has a short circuit in it and that is when they start having seizures. It usually happens during puberty, but Spencer might be getting it early. Let's not get uptight yet. Tomorrow's spinal tap will tell us if there's any infection going on in his body. I don't suspect that because he doesn't have a fever."

The possibility of epilepsy left me numb. Fighting to get past my own dread, I asked, "How long will he have seizures like these? Will they be this severe? How long will he have to be on medication? What are the side effects? How will it affect his schoolwork?" The teacher in me wanted to run to the local library and pick up a book on epilepsy.

"What would a not-so-good spinal tap show?" I asked. I wasn't sure I wanted to hear the answer.

"Well, if there's a viral or bacterial infection, the spinal fluid will come out cloudy or may have blood in it," the doctor replied confidently. I didn't want my thoughts to transfer to worry, so I changed the subject. "I must tell you that you've made this a most pleasant experience, despite the circumstances," I said. "I appreciate how well you all have taken care of us since we came in this morning. Thank you for your understanding and patience. Thank you for being here."

The doctor smiled. "You're welcome. Out here in Colby, we're not as busy as other hospitals and that helps the level of stress, considerably." Dr. Kettler was not only a pediatrician, but was also the hospital's Chief of Staff. "I'll be back in a couple of hours. I need to go mow my lawn and see *my* family for a while. Don't fret; if anything changes I'm only a few blocks away." I liked this small town nice guy!

11

Home Sweet Home

June 10, 2000

We reached our welcoming doorstep back in Colorado and into my husband's arms. Spencer's doctor here determined his discomfort stemmed from a "Dylantin hangover" that would last for another day or so. He still complained of bad headaches, which set him adrift in a fog of his own. No one could join him wherever he was; no one could reach him in there. No wonder he was frightened to be left alone. Somewhere between Colby and Denver there was a bigger problem to be resolved it seemed, so I bought a new journal to begin recording Spencer's medical condition, allergies, and his progress just in case.

Spencer was at the bottom of the stairs the next morning making his way up for breakfast after he and his siblings had enjoyed a morning of cartoons. He turned to give his brother a hug and in the midst of it, started seizing. Evan laid him expertly on the couch. He was in a full-fledged grand mal seizure now, just like the first one. Evan made an urgent call to 911.

As I was summarizing Spencer's medical problems to the dispatcher, he began throwing up and then biting his cheek. I looked up and saw sister Elle taking in this scene.

She started to cry and said, "Mommy, Spencer's hurt. There's blood coming out of his mouth." One arm was on Spencer and another consoling Elle when Evan began crying too. *Deep breath, Angie, deep breath*, echoed back to me. All of us shared the waterworks!

As calmly and as purposefully as I could, I said, "Evan, I need you to be my big helper and tell them everything I tell you. You can do it! I know you can." Evan held the phone and relayed everything known to date. *And where the heck was Russ, anyway?*

The sirens were getting louder and closer, thank God. Russ came in with the paramedics in tow. The EMT stabilized him with oxygen and checked his vitals, while getting his questions answered. I retold Spencer's history of the week's illness and hospital stay.

That day Evan and I learned the meaning of the "fight or flight" response. Evan told me that when Spencer started seizing, he wanted to run up to his room and hide under the covers. After he handled the 911 call that is exactly what he did. During crisis-induced fear, it's part of the fight-or-flight response to seek a safe place to go to find healthy outlets for stress. Oh, how I wished I could have joined him!

The paramedics decided to take Spencer to the hospital to determine the cause of the seizure. Russ and I agreed. Russ volunteered to go in the ambulance.

"I've called my mom to take care of Evan and Elle. So once she gets here, you can meet us up there. We're going to Swedish Hospital," Russ stated.

"Okay," I said. "See you there."

By now the new neighbors we hadn't met were showing up at our house, curious about the commotion. A spontaneous broadcast went out to the gathered crowd as Jan, my mother-in-law, arrived. And in minutes I was back on the road!

12

Flight for Life

June 10, 2000

On the way to the hospital I talked to my mom and sister on the phone, repeating all that had just happened. I was overcome, hyperventilating, feeling a tingling sensation traveling through my arms and felt utterly colorless; tetherless. Regaining a light foothold on some moveable and fragile surface, I called Russ. He told me Spencer had just stopped breathing in the ambulance because they gave him Valium to stop the seizure. *Oh, again!*

"They were about to intubate him but he started breathing on his own," Russ said calmly. "He's fine at this moment."

"The same thing happened in Colby," I said. "We've got to make sure they don't give him Valium again. I'll be there in about ten minutes."

"Meet us in the ER," Russ informed. "We just pulled in."

Spencer lay on the gurney, his arms and legs tied down. The little patient was very woozy from the physical mutiny. Before I had a chance to console Spencer, he was loaded onto the Flight for Life pad that was taking him to Children's Hospital in Denver.

"Is it really that serious?" I asked.

The ER doctor said, "Since we don't know what's happening with Spencer and he stopped breathing, we don't want to take the chance of another 30-to-40 minute drive in traffic. He really needs to go to Children's, as they specialize in children."

The two of us ran back to the car just as the helicopter was taking off. We looked up to see it fly over us in the parking lot. Russ drove which gave me a chance to pray away my frayed nerves.

Once we got Spencer admitted to the Children's ER, the employees seemed overly calm and nonchalant about the situation—you know, it's an E.M.E.R.G.E.N.C.Y. Hello? Is anybody in there? Yeah, yeah, I know . . . they deal with crisis every day; it's their norm. But it took nearly fifteen minutes for anyone to come into the room, and once they did, the time was spent reviewing everything that had happened since the moment it began. When the technician left, there was no discussion about what would happen next or even what they could do now. Instead he said, "If he starts to seize, come get us right away." Russ had previously served his time in the ER and in the operating room, so we were ready for it.

We waited another 30 minutes for the neurologist to arrive. During that time Spencer was quite groggy, lying on the bed dozing in and out of sleep. He would respond when we talked to him, but his reactions were lethargic, delayed, and confused.

"Good afternoon," said the tall, thin, middle-aged man who forced us out of our thoughts. "My name is Dr. Johnson and I'm a neurologist here at Children's. This must be Spencer." He spent the next half hour going over Spencer's history and conducted a neurological exam. "I think this young man is developing epilepsy. In that case we need to put him on an anti-seizure medication. There is a new drug out called Trileptol that I think he would do well with," he concluded.

"Are there any side effects of this medication? Is there a reason why he is having such a hard time talking?" We asked in turns. "Could you tell us what to expect from a child with epilepsy? How long will this last?"

Dr. Johnson promptly responded, "First of all, this medication could make him a little drowsy at first until his body gets used to it. He may have a bit of a dry mouth and constipation as well. There will be a pamphlet attached to the bottle regarding side effects. Read it for more detailed information. I have a book I'll give you on epilepsy and it explains, in a simple way, what it is and how to deal with it. And as far as speech goes, kids can have trouble with speech three hours to three days after a grand mal seizure."

"My brother has grand mal seizures, too, and his speech is only affected for a few minutes afterward," Russ said.

"Keep an eye on his speech. It should get better," he assured us. "By the 4th of July this will all be just a bad memory, right Spencer?" He patted Spencer on the shoulder. "Let me write up the prescription, get some samples and then you guys can get out of here."

"You're not going to keep him for overnight observation?" I asked. "They just flew him by helicopter from Swedish. Why would they do that if they didn't think it was *serious*?"

"He seized and then stopped breathing, so they wanted to get him here ASAP to avoid another episode or another problem or situation." The doctor went on to say, "I checked him out and he's fine. The tests have shown nothing and we can assume that it's epilepsy. Let me know how he does on the Trileptol. When they bring your release papers, you're free to go."

Russ and I exchanged glances. He assured me the doctor was right and we could go.

Something nagged at me and swirled around my thoughts; I was realizing that the journal I bought had not yet been opened! So I summoned any available energy to pen a thorough account of all that we knew to date. At least then we would KNOW if Spencer improved and by how much.

13

Many Signs, No Answers

June 10, 2000

Spencer slept all the way home from the hospital, which gave the two of us a chance to talk. Wanting to protect me, Russ tried to play down the worst of my fears. We would start Spencer on the Trileptol and see how things progressed with the hope that he would improve.

Spencer loved checkers, so when we got home, I asked if he'd like to play. Maybe a little enjoyable activity might take his mind off the pain. He looked tattered and disheveled, but he agreed. As we played, he had to lie down, complaining that the back of his head hurt when he sat up. He could feel his heart beating behind his ears. "Throbbing?" I inquired, and he nodded. Then he pointed to his right temple and said it hurt there this morning before his seizure. He moved and spoke slowly, his spirit waning to a ghost-likeness, displaying the garbled effects that mark a seizure. He didn't want to play anymore.

I choked back my tears. It was difficult to see him in so much pain. In my heart I knew we were losing our little boy.

That night he ate a good dinner and we started him on the Trileptol. Spencer was on a makeshift bed on the floor of our bedroom where he half-slept all night. He'd wake up shouting gibberish, "a-y-a-yay-ya-y-y-a-yyay-y-a-y." Then he'd throw his hands up in the air a couple of times and fall back to sleep. Sometimes he would wake up crying, holding his head, yell for us and doze back off. Just as I would settle myself back down and fall alseep, he would wake up, starting it all over again.

Come Sunday, we were wholly exhausted by the 24-hour (and counting) rollercoaster ride. Spencer woke to a severe ache pointing to his forehead once more. His eyes hurt, he was highly sensitive to light and his speech was worse than before. Debating whether to take him back to the hospital or not, Russ suggested we wait it out on the medicine a little longer.

A seriously groggy, disoriented, and confused Spencer stuttered, "Mom, the toilet is...the toilet is...the toilet is..."

"Clogged?" I asked.

He was having a hard time recalling words like they were lost. It was as if his brain would start a thought process, but somewhere along the way the connection was undone and the thought was dropped.

Migraines produce slurred speech, but memory loss too? Lost words? Was this in fact just epilepsy? Side effects of the Trileptol?

When we gave him Motrin for the headaches we waited for it to take effect so the confusion would mostly clear and he could talk again. When the pain let up, he was like a new person. Guessing there might be more to this—or that someone could have overlooked something—we turned to the best encyclopedia we knew, the Internet.

The list of side effects for Trileptol include:

dizziness, drowsiness, headache, vision changes, double vision, excessive tiredness, upset stomach, vomiting, tremors, difficulty coordinating movement, speech problems, difficulty concentrating, nervousness, and confusion.

That pretty much described Spencer for the time being, except for the vomiting. Is it common to display these side effects after only two doses? The Valium hit him immediately, and two times, so yes it would seem possible.

I wondered why a doctor would give that drug with all those side effects. Could it be better than the seizure itself? After discussing all our concerns with a new doctor, we agreed that it was time to bring Spencer back to Children's for more tests. Far be it from me to question anyone about the life and death of my own son. *And another question . . . did he really have epilepsy?*

14

Soap Opera Drama

June 11, 2000

We had just spent two more hours in the ER and then got settled into a room. I agreed to stay overnight with Spencer while Russ decided to be home with Evan and Elle. The three of us looked every part of lifeless and shattered. With the late hour, it was too far into the afternoon to do any tests and we would have to wait until morning. The counterbalance to this would be for the *medical staff* to observe Spencer's inexplicable behavior.

By 4:30 p.m., Spencer began to have a headache that intensified to the point where he did not want to speak. He complained of sharp pains behind his right eye and temple. When the pain came, he jerked his arms up, reached for his head and began to cry. Each cry of pain sent a jab to my heart. At 4:50 p.m. we gave Spence Ibuprofen, and by 5:20 his pain was decreasing. By 5:30 he was asleep. Peace.

While Spencer dozed, I prayed to find the "off" switch to this ride. *It's summer, I just want to take my kids to the pool.* Spencer's nap was short. By 6:00 he was awake and ready for pizza. He spent some time looking at books and watching

TV before he became sleepy again. He was getting tired of me interrogating him with the same questions.

"Do you have a headache? Where does it hurt? Can you see me okay? How does the rest of your body feel? Are you sick to your stomach? Do you want something to eat or drink?" *Did I sense that his speech would not last much longer?* I had to get as much information as quickly as I could.

At 8:00 p.m. he was asleep again, so I took the opportunity to make phone calls and catch everyone up on the latest. At 9:20, Spencer was twitching his lips, chin, and right arm in his sleep. This was *not* normal. I laid my hand on his chest and gently woke him. I asked if he still had a headache and he said that he did. An additional dose of Motrin gave him a chance to sleep through the night. I slept beside him.

We shared the room that night with an eighteen-month-old girl who had a rare disease. Grandma and Great Grandma were with her. This family was from Wyoming and this was the closest children's hospital. They were in Colorado for a routine four-month visit to do specific tests and treatments on this little angel. These women softened my mind of worry and diffused the frustration I felt toward the medical staff. They radiated pure love and compassion.

Their whole scenario became a bit of soap opera drama. Their ordeal seemed so much worse. As I lay in our single bed, I prayed and dozed.

Around 5 a.m., the ringing phone startled me awake.

Grandma picked up. "Hello?"

Silence…long silence. Heavy breathing, whimpers, "No! No!" Hysterical sobbing ensued.

Grandma slammed the phone down. She continued crying and screaming colorful metaphors. She seemed to fly through all three stages of denial, anger, and sadness within a few minutes. Selfishly, I lay there hoping Spencer would not wake up.

Finally, Grandma shared the conversation with her mother. Her brother had taken his own life during the night. The person whom she had just spoken to, walked out into the garage to see why the dogs were barking, and found him. Tears soaked my pillow. I cried for them and Spencer. I just wanted everything to be okay. Was this all a bad dream?

I offered my condolences and we exchanged addresses. Over the weeks, I prayed that their situation was getting better, as ours grew worse, but I never heard from them again.

15

A Prayer Answered

June 12, 2000

By 10:30 a.m. Spencer was skinny from fasting and looked like an alien. He was lying on his bed with probes sticking out all over his head. This EEG would hopefully show something more enlightening than the first one six days before. Spencer was lying very still as the technician had instructed. After an hour of looking at the brain waves, we would be going down to get an MRI and then be on our way home. These tests were to confirm the diagnosis of epilepsy with certainty. Upon returning from the EEG, Spencer complained that he was still hungry.

I walked up to the nurses' station where our favorite day nurse was reading a chart. Angelina was doing paperwork. "Excuse me Angelina," I said.

She looked up and flashed me the "just one second" gesture as she hurried away. "Yes, what can I help you with?" she said as she walked back.

"I was wondering how much longer you think it will be until Spencer's MRI. He's famished," I said.

"Funny you asked, I just called down there and they informed me that they have had two emergency MRIs this morning. They are pretty backed up and said we probably could not get to him until 4 o'clock."

Some time in the early evening, the technician came in with the EEG results that showed nothing more than irregular brainwaves. "These confirmed signs of seizure activity being controlled by Trileptol," he confirmed. I asked the technician if he would compare these EEG results to those from Colby. He later returned to say they were very similar. Again the diagnosis was epilepsy.

REALLY??? I think I've learned more about epilepsy from the Internet this last week and I'm sure it's NOT EPILEPSY for heaven's sake! I protested, unsaid. I felt wrought with suspicion because it didn't fit like a well-played jigsaw puzzle. I then christened myself Spencer's chief executive medical officer.

I couldn't wrap my mind around a four-hour wait for the MRI. How can I calm Spencer down and distract him from feeling hungry? Right about then Russ walked in and we were glad and quite relieved to see him. I left and went down to MRI on the first floor. When the person at the desk greeted me, I stated that my son is up on the third floor and we've been waiting on an MRI since last night. I asked if it will happen soon to figure out whether to wait or go home and come back tomorrow. Can't seem to get any relief!

She told me I could go down the hall and ask the technicians where he was on the list. I walked through the double doors and came to a group dressed in scrubs. I stood there smiling, not knowing who to talk to. Awkwardly I said, "Excuse me for interrupting, but my son is up on the third floor waiting for an MRI. He's very hungry because we've been here waiting since last night. If it's going to be much longer, we might need to feed him, go home and come back tomorrow."

"What's his name?" a woman asked. She was looking at me, a little confused about the fact that some mom from upstairs was standing in front of her.

"Spencer McCombs," I replied. She looked at the chart on the wall and said, "Oh, he's next. You can bring him down." I was relieved. "Well there was one answer to prayer," I said.

When I arrived back at the nurses' station, I asked for Angelina. She came walking out of the staff room with spaghetti hanging out of her mouth. I was feeling bold, so I just smiled and asked, "May I have Spencer's chart?"

"His chart?" she mumbled.

"Yes. Spencer's chart, please."

"May I ask why?"

"Sure. I was just down in MRI to ask when he might get his test done. They said he was next and to bring him down."

Surprised, she said, "Oh, okay. Well, do you need help taking him down?"

"No thanks. My husband just got here and he can help me," I said. Then Angelina, looking over her shoulder, hesitantly handed me Spencer's file. I walked back to our room and said, "Come on, we're going down to MRI." Russ looked up and rolled his eyes, thinking I was joking. "Seriously, I just talked to them. They said Spencer was next."

16

Little Tin Soldier

June 12, 2000

"Remember the Little Tin Soldier, Buggy? How stiff and brave he was?"

"Yes, Mom."

"I want you to be just like him. Be ever so still and don't move or they will have to do the test over again. When you want to move, just tell yourself, 'I AM the Little Tin Soldier and keep focused on your movie."

"Okay, Mom."

I was trying to eliminate any possibility of this MRI not working out and having to do it all over again, which somehow would probably extend to days after that. How do you get the seriousness of "lay still" across to a six-year-old boy? I assured Spencer that I'd be right there on the other side of the MRI machine within earshot if he needed anything.

As Russ and I sat anxiously waiting for the results I turned to him and asked, "If Spencer had a brain tumor, would it show up on the MRI?"

"Yes," he answered. "You would see a dark mass of tissue on the picture of the brain. I don't believe that is the problem,

ANGELA DEE

though." There again, Russ' optimism had a way of balancing
out my pessimism and I loved him for that.

Russ worked in the medical field from the time he
was 22 as an ER technician and then spent eight years,
post-graduate, in the OR operating the heart/lung machine
during open-heart surgery. He respects and trusts medical
practitioners first hand. I only had a mother's intuition and
asked questions based on gut instinct and worry. Russ believed
that I was wasting their time, but I hoped he—at some
point—would begin to trust *me*.

Our differences in dealing with medical staff, was a
strain on our relationship. I respected the doctors' training
but could not understand their lack of patience, empathy or
understanding at times. When they seemed annoyed by my
persistent questions, I'd ask more questions. I guess I just
needed answers. Russ often gave me that "you can lay off
now" look and I would back down. He may have thought
I was being rude or not respecting their time. I viewed my
persistence as a mother gaining more knowledge to work
with. Russ was among their favorites, as he was able to talk
in medical lingo and keep discussions short and to the point.
This stressor became a challenge in the weeks to come as I
tried to become less emotional and more scientific and he
tried to understand my mother's intuition.

"We're done," said the MRI technician. "You can take
Spencer back upstairs and the doctor will be up to share the
results with you when he is done with his rounds."

Once up in the room, we ordered room service. While
Spence was eating, the doctor came to reaffirm his epilepsy
diagnosis, as the MRI showed a normal brain. *Normal!? You
gotta be kidding me,* the voice in my mind replied. With it was
an intuition that wormed its way in there as well. Although
Epilepsy was manageable and I now desperately wanted to

believe this "easier" diagnosis was official and then be done with it altogether, I felt in my gut the doctor had to be wrong. Maybe dead wrong!

17

Last Kiss

June 12, 2000

After the chaos, I was relieved to see Elle and Evan at home sweet home! *Breathe it in*, I noted. I tried to be joyful through their bedtime routine and not show any signs of trouble. Evan asked about Spencer's condition. I was brief with details, but it appeared that he already intuited that there was a serious problem. He had observed Spencer's behavior over the last week. Evan had all he could handle for one night and went off to bed. It was his way of saying, "If we don't talk about it anymore, maybe it will go away."

After all, it was the beginning of summer vacation and Spencer's problem was cutting into pool time. Did Evan sense that he was losing his brother? The human heart is fragile and denial is God's way of protecting us until we can handle more. Though there was an underlying current of uncertainty with our boy who was progressing into neurological dysfunction, home felt safe; normal.

As I read Elle her bedtime story, Spencer, who had already been tucked in, began to shriek uncontrollably. I went in to check on him and he spoke in two and three word phrases in his newly developed frightened and frustrated otherworld. Whatever invisible restraints held him together at the hospital were now eroding . . . and fast!

It took us about a half an hour of yes and no questions to understand that he wanted to sleep in Mom and Dad's room. There were no words, just head nods and shakes. As Russ and I gathered his pillow and blanket, Spencer frantically walked back and forth between his room and Elle's. He walked up to me to say something, but the words would not come. He tried to speak, but it was as if his brain froze mid-sentence or on a word and he was left with his mouth open. He sighed and tried again. The thought was not even coming out halfway, like before. *Lord, give me strength to watch my ailing son.* And then it became clear that he wanted to hug and kiss his sister good night.

"Elle, can you come to the door? Spencer wants to give you a hug and kiss," I said. Elle walked to the doorway and Spencer bent over and kissed her forehead. It was one of the sweetest moments. Her big green eyes lit up with a smile (Spencer rarely gave *anyone* kisses, being a germophobe). Then he wrapped his arms around her and seemed not to want to let her go. Elle's chubby little arms held Spencer tightly and they rocked back and forth until Spencer was able to walk away. I stepped into Spencer's room to regain my composure. This was a supernatural moment for us, for the journal, too. Spencer would not be able to hug or kiss his sister ever again. She would not remember it, but I would remember it forever.

18

Losing Minds

June 13, 2000

When Spencer woke from relentless restless nights, he was rubbing his tongue and teeth with his fingers. He was only able to utter two or three words at a time. It was an odd thought that maybe his mouth was going numb. He was also gritting his teeth. On top of all that, he was struggling with a lot of gas and diarrhea. He was getting migraine headaches  off and on, managed only slightly by alternating between Tylenol and Motrin. When asked to squeeze my finger, he couldn't.

In the throes of a migraine, he had to lie flat, motionless, and not be touched. He told me that his forehead and the base of his skull hurt. His eyes hurt and he squinted painfully. He'd jerk his hand up to cover his eyes as he moaned in pain.

I asked if it felt like pins were sticking in his eyes and he nodded "Yes." As he grabbed his eyes, he rolled from side to side in agony, screaming then crying. At times, he would reach up with his hands and scratch toward the ceiling as if hallucinating. He yelled, "Mom!" persistently. I reassured him I was right there, and he'd reached over to the side that was *empty* seeking my hand.

So many emotions welled up inside of me. Just when neither one of *us* could withstand any more, the Motrin would kick in and he'd fall asleep. The migraines continued through the next day. Now he was only able to say "Mom" followed by a very frustrated "Oh" because he couldn't say what he wanted to. The frustration and loss of words turned to a "ja ja ja ja, ya ya ya ya" gibberish that he would randomly blurt out.

He pointed to things, which led us to ask questions that he could not respond to. Sometimes we could make out what he was trying to tell us, and other times it made no sense at all. After sipping soup for lunch, his eyes rolled back, his chin began to vibrate, he started to grit his teeth and his right arm trembled. Another seizure had come lasting six minutes. This was the first seizure since we had put him on the Trileptol. The result of a phone call to the neurologist was an increased dosage of the drug.

Spencer's mind was coming undone—literally—and there wasn't anything anybody could do about it! This fact seemed all too obvious to me, but those around me thought it was me who was sliding into the abyss. My growing fear prompted me to search my thoughts. To come up with just *one* person who could be convinced—to see what I see—to see that Spencer is not okay by any measure. Gratefully, my parents and my friend Kris alternated to help me for the rest of the week while Russ was busy with work.

19

Laughing Is Easier

June 14, 2000

"Angie, could you come here, please?" Kris raised her voice from our bedroom. "I think Spencer has to use the potty." I looked down to see him struggling to get out of bed. He got up and proceeded to walk into the hallway. It looked as if he'd just had a stroke as he was clenching his fist and releasing it, tapping out his S.O.S., he was dragging his right leg behind him. His right arm was bent with a hand that was making palsy-like movements. When Spencer got to the foyer he stopped, looked up at the ceiling, staggered to keep his balance and then appeared to be lost. Then he proceeded to urinate all over himself.

With pee running down his leg, Kris and I looked at one another in shock, as two worried mothers would do. Kris promptly tried to move the situation along so she wouldn't have to stand there and watch me slip into despair. Spencer did the Thorazine shuffle to the bathroom and Kris helped him onto the toilet. The whole time, my Buggy acted as if nothing had happened, his face flat and void of emotion. Had my normal Spencer just peed all over himself, he would be rushing to shower right away, crying and embarrassed beyond belief. When Spencer sat on the toilet, he lost control of his body and sank into the hole. With his rear end in the water, he began laughing uncontrollably and so did we. Sometimes people laugh instead of cry; it's easier to laugh.

We got him cleaned up and back to bed. Kris fed Spencer a piece of sweet roll and juice as he could no longer manage the fine motor skills of his arms and hands. His body was actively deteriorating and I couldn't bear it!

That night I wrote in the journal, "Overall bad day for Spencer: two seizures. He went from a 3 or 4-year-old's functioning to an infant level overnight. Out of my mind with worry." He was literally acting like a well-practiced drunk, wasted beyond function. His words were not even slurred anymore; there was nothing but gibberish now. Kris and I both knew that he was not going to wake up the next morning mostly normal, with a few less brain cells and a big headache. While Kris kept feeding Spencer, it became most evident to her that we had to get him back to the hospital without delay.

I stood at the doorway watching Spencer fall back to sleep while Kris rubbed his back. The rush of tears broke the dam. Kris came to the door and moved me into the hall, shutting the door behind her. "Angie, this is serious. I didn't know how bad Spencer was until I came to help you today. You have got to get him back to the hospital. Something is terribly wrong and I urge you to call Russ right now. He needs to be here with you."

When Kris, my Little Mary Sunshine childhood friend, told me it was SERIOUS, it confirmed what I knew in my gut: *Yes. Hell yes! This IS serious!* Any small bit of denial now vanished. Any submission or compliance to those doctors' even keel flushed down with it too. And our fight was about to take flight!

Knowing Kris since we were both fourteen, we had been through a lot together: junior high with bad hair, high school and silly boys, college with smarter boys, weddings, and now kids in all their splendor! Through it all, she was the optimistic one, trudging forward, overcoming obstacles, persevering, making the most out of life and laughing all the way. I had not remembered a day in our friendship when we did not share a belly laugh or two. On this day, Kris' signature perky dimples now looked like hollows of sadness. There were no girly delights in this day. I knew it was time to call Russ and then my parents.

20

Seriously?

June 15, 2000

I called Russ with Kris standing in the hallway. I told him briefly about the day, trying to be calm. My voice quivered.

"I have to run to the bank to make a deposit, get gas, and then I'll be home," Russ said.

"No, Russ. You don't understand. I need you NOW. Not in ten minutes, not in 20 minutes, not in 30 minutes. NOW! As in, maybe *yesterday* . . . and *last week* too. I need you *now*." My sobs escaped without permission and my anger erupted. I'm sure if Kris were looking at my temples, she would have seen my pulse beating wildly, ready to explode. I was wholly exhausted, emotionally and physically.

Russ was the indifferent one during times of crisis. It makes sense. Russ' biggest fear in life was to have a disabled child. He grew up with one brother, five years older, who had cerebral palsy and a mental handicap. Though their family made the best of their situation, his brother, Will, was a drain on his parents' finances, an added stress to their relationship. Through no fault of his own he kept them from life's big adventures, vacations, and activities. Russ could not help but think how his life would have been different with a normal older brother. Russ played two roles growing up—being both the big *and* little brother. Expectations for him were high, because he was the "normal son" and Russ never wanted to disappoint or bring additional drama to his family.

When Russ had three healthy, normal children, he was relieved more than I ever knew. He thanked God that he did not have to worry about his worst nightmare any longer. When I called for help on this day, stalling was his way of saying, "It's not that bad. In fact, maybe this is not really happening." Russ was placing a filter on his heart so he did not have to take on *this* reality, the pain of retracing his own steps. All I knew is that he could not be away anymore, leaving me to do this on my own.

On Friday, my parents spent the day at our house and confirmed everything Kris had said. I knew we would be going back to the hospital for an extended stay as soon as we could convince the doctors to reassess Spencer's diagnosis.

When my parents walked in the door, Spencer ran to his grandma. She picked him up and held him tightly. He clung to her, laying his head on her shoulder. It was like he was telling her, *Please figure this out, Grandma; no one else seems to know what is happening to me.* My mother, who I had rarely seen cry, couldn't hold it back. She embraced Spencer until her curiosity got the best of her. She set him down to allow him to be on his own footing for a better view. They were now seeing how his neurological functioning had degraded over the past 48 hours. Russ was asking Spencer questions repetitively, trying to prove to us that it was not as bad as we thought. The more we tuned in, the worse it got. Spencer's inability to speak turned into frustrated babbling and crying. Seeing my parents' reactions fueled my fear and there was no place for it to hide. A spark of genius fired Russ as he grabbed the video camera and started filming to document Spencer's decline.

And then it happened. That moment that Spencer lost it and all the dominoes began to lean too far to one side. He kept pointing to the sliding glass door that led to the backyard. (He pointed at everything now, because his speech was gone). We asked him if he wanted to go see the dog. He dragged his stiff right leg as he sidestepped with his left leg to go outside on the back porch. Spencer stood there and looked around like he had to familiarize himself with this place. Then he marched awkwardly to the end of the deck and stared back, facing into the family room windows, conjuring up an image of our senile dog, which would go outside, turn around, look back in, then scratch on the door, forgetting why she went out in the first place. The strange, unnatural scene was proof that Spencer was not operating well; I went outside to guide him back in.

My parents helped us get Spencer to bed and then gave us the same serious talk that Kris had done the day before. I was glad Russ was there to hear it. I phoned the neurologist on call and he informed me that we could come to the hospital, but no doctors would be available to look at him until the next day. We would just be losing another night's sleep and we'd be better off waiting until morning. *As if we were sleeping at home anymore?*

My mom suggested that we call a priest so that he could come over and perform the Sacrament of Last Rights. These are prayers over a person before they die and can only be administered by a priest. We were *so* frightened that Spencer would not make it through the night. When the priest called back and found out that Spencer was asleep, he suggested that we wait until morning. Seriously?!

PART III

ROUGH SEAS

"We are holding on to the hope of God's promises as an anchor for the soul, firm and secure.
Hebrews 6:19

21

Wedding Anniversary

June 16, 2000

"Okay. (sigh) Well I think we are ready again," I reported. I had finally gotten Spencer dressed. He fought me the whole time. That little booger was strong and I felt like I just finished a wrestling match. Even though his brain was wackadoo, he still understood that we were going back to the hospital. I glanced over at my sister, Carmen, who was sitting on my kitchen floor unpacking china boxes. It had been less than a month since we moved into our new house. My older sister—floodgates open, unashamed and unrestrained—was always a pillar of strength for me, the June Cleaver of the clan. It had all caught up with her too.

"It's your tenth wedding anniversary and it dawned on me that I am unpacking your china for the first time since your wedding. And you're heading back to the hospital. This is not the way it is supposed to be." She shook her head slightly. "Your wedding day was so beautiful, perfect. This day is so different. I would have never imagined."

I had forgotten all about our anniversary and right now it seemed so insignificant. We would be cancelling our renewal of vows celebration that was to take place in our flower garden.

"I never imagined anything like this happening when we decided to have kids. I'm not sure I signed up for this, did I?" I walked over and gave Carmen a hug and thanked her for coming to watch the kids. One lone tear fell and I wiped it away. I had to get Spencer back to Children's.

"Erin, do you want to go with Angie and Russ in case they need help?" Carmen asked her daughter. Sweet and shy Erin was fifteen when she last shared a dance with her cousin Spencer at the wedding on his birthday.

"*S u r e . . .* I guess," she said tentatively, not knowing what to say. The look on her face spelled out the opposite, but she was trying to please her mom; to be agreeable. Having Erin witness Spencer's decent with *her* degree of connection to him, was asking too much. She volunteered anyway.

Russ carried Spencer to the car and he started to kick and scream so wildly that it took all three of us to get him in the car. Spencer was shoving his legs into the air and flailing his arms, thrashing from one side of the truck to the other, scratching at the doors, howling and bawling. This went on for ten minutes. "Geez Bug, chill out!" I muttered. It was peculiar to see some old behaviors like a temper tantrum in the current Spencer . . . like they didn't go together or even know each other anymore.

When he moved to the door and started picking at the locks to pull them up, it became obvious that he couldn't decipher where the locks were or how to operate them. He threw all his energy into the mission. He did NOT WANT TO GO BACK TO THE HOSPITAL! It couldn't be helped, we *knew*, so we managed to get him buckled in and tamed enough to be on our way. Reversing to the end of the driveway, with a clear picture of Erin in view, was earth shattering to see how shaken she had become. When she was offered an option to stay here because *we* could handle Spencer, she bolted to the security of her mom. *I want* my *mom*, I thought.

Spencer was lying in my arms like a rag doll, totally zoned out upon arriving at the hospital. It was Saturday and the ER was full. Nevertheless, they seemed to recognize Spencer as a priority and we got in pretty quickly. *Thank-you God!* We filled in the new resident who had just begun his two-week rotation. Another hour was spent giving detailed information and answering many questions. I was becoming quite efficient at telling the condensed version and I promised myself I would write it up in bullet points and hand it to the next doctor who asked his history. Maybe that would save time and heartache from retelling the story so many times. And after all, I am his Chief Executive Medical Officer! This resident looked young enough to be my son.

Suddenly Spencer shot up and pointed to the TV, babbling at the cartoons. He wriggled around on the bed and giggled as if he had ants in his pants. This energy burst usually came before a seizure. He had had enough of them now that a pattern was emerging. Not three minutes later, Spencer started his worst grand mal seizure ever. With a jolt, I ran out to find the doctor. The front desk was alerted and a minute later our resident came running in. By the time the seizure was at three minutes, ten medical personnel were standing there observing our boy. They intubated him to help him breathe, as he was not breathing on his own. The seizure went on for the longest 12 minutes (TWELVE WHOLE MINUTES FOR CRYING OUT LOUD!) Ativan was administered to stop it. This seizure caught the neurologist's attention. *Yes!* They finally had to look beyond the diagnosis of epilepsy.

When terror had convinced me that this was IT—that Spencer was going to die—I ran to get the hospital chaplain. He was sitting at his desk writing. I poked my head in and said, "Excuse me, my son is in the ER and is having a bad seizure that may not stop. Would you help me pray for him?"

"I'm finishing up some wedding plans right now. I'll be there in a few minutes." He said without even looking up.

In a few minutes he could be gone, I thought. I was so shocked by his response that I walked away in a daze. *Paralyzed*. I headed back to the ER and learned they had given Spencer meds and the seizure was slowing. A seizure like *that* was comparable to running a double marathon! I glanced over at Russ. I wondered if his insides were churning like mine. How could he be so calm and unaffected like the chaplain? He sat at the foot of the bed the whole time, timing Spencer's seizure. *Talk about cool. Frozen?* I searched before I came to it: *Experienced. Separating emotion from science. I wish I could do that!* I stuck my head outside for a swallow of unfamiliar air and perhaps to see if the chaplain was coming after all. He never showed up.

22

The Diagnosis

June 16, 2000

"Well, the MRI came out normal once again," the doctor explained, "Though there are no signs of swelling or damage, I believe that the neurological downturn we have seen over the last two weeks is indicative of viral encephalitis. His behaviors are following the course of illness we would expect to see in encephalitis patients."

Finally a diagnosis other than the one I'd fought for two weeks. "Can you explain what this means?" I asked.

"A virus has gotten into Spencer's brain. He got a virus like so many of us do every day, but our immune system fights them off. Spencer's immune system was low, and the virus crossed the blood brain barrier. If it is in fact a virus, it will have to run its course. Only bacterial encephalitis will respond to antibiotics." Dr. Pearson held a calm demeanor that felt soothing to be around.

I looked over at my husband who was sitting there speechless. "So, what are we looking at?" His code for, give me as much information as possible without all the fluff.

"My guess is that he may have a gastro intestinal virus or possibly West Nile. Typically, a child Spencer's age fairs pretty well in the recovery process. If he were a baby, he would not have as good of a chance because the brain is still developing rapidly and there is no established memory. Spencer is in the best age group for a quick recovery. He will probably exhibit similar behaviors like he's had for another week or so and *then* begin to slowly get better. His speech and emotions will be the last to come back. Kids with encephalitis can be in the hospital for a few days up to three weeks. We will do more tests in the morning to determine the virus." The doctor concluded on a positive note.

Dr. Pearson was trying to tame the monster of fear that plagued our faces.

We prayed for a quick recovery and we focused on the best possible outcome. I'd be scouring the internet for information on encephalitis, tonight. Three weeks in Children's Hospital sounded like an eternity!

Our good friends, Tami and Josh, had just shown up to celebrate our tenth wedding anniversary. After all, they were our matchmakers, introducing us in college. We engaged them in our current family drama while enjoying a Mexican dinner. Josh was upbeat and encouraging, as always. He was his goofy self. Tami brought up some old memories that we reminisced about. Good times. The laughter lifted our moods and everything returned to the way we used to be. Swirling questions were sitting in my mind waiting to be released, but they would have to wait until morning. Russ suggested I go home and get some rest and he would stay with Spencer tonight.

On the road home, the rain came down in a torrent. I had my wipers on high and I noticed my gas gauge was on empty. I pushed the button for the mileage meter and 34 miles blinked in red LED light. I decided to chance it. My exhaustion exceeded the need to stop for gas. Besides, it couldn't be many more miles from downtown, right? I asked God to get me home safely without falling asleep, running on fumes, to be left stranded. About halfway home I pushed the mileage button again, but the numbers did not appear. Aggravated, I repeatedly pushed the button. Each time I pushed, this voice in my head said, "Do you trust me? Do you trust me? Do you trust me?" It was like one of those squeaky toys. *The squeak is the same the first time AND the tenth time so why do we always have to squeeze it again?* I stopped pushing the button and let God lead the way.

"Yes, Lord, I trust you." I said aloud.

"Then focus on driving," God said.

Oh wait! God, you're talking to me. As the rain plastered the windshield, passing cars sent walls of water into the side of my van and I could barely see the road. Tension made me throttle that button again to take my mind off of driving. This time the number 34 lit up *again. Wait a minute now. I've gone close to 25 miles...what's wrong with this thing?*

"Do you trust me?" I heard again.

I measured the distance with the odometer. I went two more miles, pushed the button and the light flashed 28. *I did not just go 6 miles. This thing is messing with me!* I laughed.

I went another five miles and the light read 19, then two miles and the light read 11, another two and 6 lit up. By the time I drove into my driveway it flashed 0. I laughed out loud, "I think God has a sense of humor."

When I relayed this story to my husband he said, "Oh, you would not have run out of gas anyway. You have another 30-40 miles after the reading is at 0.

"Well, if that were true, then why did it not start this morning? I tried three times before I asked, 'God could you please just get me to the gas station?' The fourth time it started."

Russ shrugged his shoulders. "Who knows?"

Come on, have a little faith, Babe. I thought.

Maybe Russ was right, but I still believed God was giving me a lesson in trust. If I could trust God with the little requests, maybe eventually I could trust God with prayers that seemed impossible.

23

Incredible Hulk

June 17, 2000

Russ had just spent his first twenty-four hours with Spencer since all of this had begun and he'd come to a better understanding of what we had undergone the past two weeks. Some of Spencer's episodes had been so bizarre. I'd tried to explain, but he didn't seem to believe it. I'm not sure I would have understood it either. If seeing is believing, then we'll soon join forces.

When I walked in, Russ was on the makeshift bed rocking our Spencer Lee. Our eyes met and instantly I knew everything was sinking in. He lay Spencer down and we hugged. His tears came. "I don't know how you've done it these few weeks. I am utterly spent, emotionally and physically."

Resentment was what I felt first, but then I softened to say, "I understand. I have done it only because I had to. Any mother would." We held each other for a few minutes hoping it would all go away.

I had a feeling this crisis would make us or break us. For our kids' sake, we needed to stay together. God would be our strong tower, miracle worker, sustaining force.

"Well I've learned one thing since I've been laying here awake all night," said Russ. "Never take your family for granted. Life can change in an instant. And last night was mayhem." We shared unguarded tears.

With the virus attacking the part of the brain that controls emotions, it had been another night of fits of rage. Spencer had gone into an "Incredible Hulk" temper tantrum around 2 a.m., stood up on his bed, and fell off. Russ then requested a bed on the floor with padded walls around it… roughing out a makeshift Craig Bed. Russ had explained to the nurses that others would not be able to handle his strength when enraged, so he put Spencer in a safer sleeping arrangement on the floor. What a sight!

After we finished lunch, the chaplain walked in to pray with us. *This* woman was loving and kind. It was obvious that she had a heart for the Lord and her compassion washed away all traces of disappointment with the chaplain from the day before. My brother Brad, his wife Michele, and daughter Kate had brought us lunch. We had just filled them in on the diagnosis. The prayer calmed all of us and restored our hope.

Russ was anxious to get home. "I've got to get some sleep. Call me when you are leaving and I will come to relieve you."

"My mom is coming to relieve me so we both can sleep tonight." I said.

"Ooooh, goooood. Thank God!" Russ sighed contentedly as he walked out the door.

24

Daydream

June 17, 2000

Spencer awoke and unpre-dictably sat up in bed. "Hi. How ya doin' Bud?" I asked.

"Hi, good," he answered clearly, to my amazement.

What a reward. With each small step to recovery, he restored expectation. I'd think to myself, *the virus has run its course and we are closer to going home.* My mind drifted into a daydream. Spencer was running around the last corner

of the mile relay with a hundred meters to go—achy muscles and burning lungs—he'd rev up what he had left and let the wind at his back push him faster toward the finish line. I prayed he was running through ribbons.

Spencer seemed to display his most normal behaviors right after waking up. Then, when his brain had time to catch up, he started acting silly again. His behavior that day included restlessness, kicking, straightening his arms for no apparent reason, excessive saliva that he had trouble swallowing, and dilated pupils. His face twitched continuously, and he was grinding his teeth. The scene from the rabid dog in the movie *Old Yeller* flashed across my consciousness. I felt ashamed, but this child in front of me was not the son I once knew.

Newsflash: The hospital had wagons! So Spencer and I tried a wagon ride around the hall. Spencer had clumsily tried to crawl out of the wagon several times and was ripping off his diaper. He might have known, somehow, that a six-year-old should not be wearing a diaper and didn't want to be associated with the thing. It seemed that even though his mind was not quite right, he had pride in his manhood. He just did not have the ability to express it verbally. When we got back, he went to the bathroom like a big boy.

I was dead on my feet, a walking zombie and looked it. I found myself staring at the five Field Day ribbons Spencer had won three weeks earlier. Four first place and one second place ribbon. The blue and red ribbons were accompanied by pictures of our family, along with cards and crayon drawings from loved ones taped all over the side of his "padded cell".

My thoughts rewound to Field Day and I closed my eyes to relive it. We were at the starting line of the shoe toss and Spencer was handing me his shoe to get the shoelace loosened just right. Then he grabbed it and ran to where the other boys were already lined up. The teacher took her spot, ready to start. Spencer asked the teacher if she could hang on just one minute. He did not have his foot placed in the shoe quite right in order to "flip a good zinger" as he'd put it.

"Kick it low and far, Buggy," I coached. He gave me a crusty look then nodded at the teacher, letting her know he was ready. *I should know better than to call him Buggy in front of his friends,* I realized too late. After all, he is going to be a big first grader next year.

The teacher cried, "On your marks…get set…KICK!" Spencer gave it all the zing he could and by the determined look on his face I just knew that his navy blue shoe had sailed beyond the rest. I saw it land.

The teacher announced 1st, 2nd, and 3rd place, and the next thing I knew, Spencer was running my way to show off his blue ribbon. "Good job, Spence." I gave him a big hug.

He won three more ribbons that day including a blue ribbon for the three-legged-race with his friend Peter. The two pals had practiced just enough to get their tied legs in sync, so they would not fall or waste time. It worked! He won another ribbon on the team Slip and Slide, where he pulled his friends down a water slide on a tube. The best time won. He was pulling kids twice his weight. Spencer was a skinny little thing but determined and highly competitive. The last event was the Balloon Toss. His tosses went far, but landed gently. I thought the balloon would never break. He and Peter played for several minutes after all the other balloons had exploded. Everyone was cheering for them. Then proudly they accepted their ribbons. Milestones!

Nurse Tarin walked in with a squealing Spencer and snapped me out of my daydream. Field Day had been less than a month ago. I wished we could go back in time to that day and have the wisdom to know how to stop the virus from traveling to his brain. I lay with him rubbing his back until he fell asleep. I wanted my little boy back. Rewind me please.

25

Boggled Mind

June 17, 2000

Down in the hospital cafeteria I was walking around in a dull, witless state. My body was tired from the constant emotional upheaval. I couldn't make any more decisions, not even a simple one, like what to eat. I had no appetite and in two weeks I had dropped ten pounds. I quickly grabbed a stale piece of pizza, some juice, paid for it, and sat down to eat. As I ate, the events of the last two weeks raced through my own cerebral matter followed by persistent mind chatter. I reviewed every minute I could account for to figure when and where Spencer would have contracted whatever was in his brain.

Okay, the doctors say the incubation period is ten days to two weeks. What were we doing two weeks ago? Russ took the boys to Chatfield Reservoir for that Boy Scouting Day. But they've already determined it's not the virus from a mosquito. Did he drink some bad water? Did Spencer act sick on Field Day? He was rather bearish and impatient from the move and end of school year activities. Remember the intermittent blinking? Could that have been evidence of blurred vision and headaches? And then I heard myself proclaim, "Oh my goodness, the strep throat!"

Spencer was a strep carrier every year without many symptoms. Chronic ear infections as a baby made Spencer more prone to illness than our other two kids. Being on so many antibiotics as a baby, he built up a resistance to them, and it weakened his immune system. Only the stronger antibiotics seemed to work on him now. Spencer had strep in his body from March to May this year. After two weeks of each antibiotic, we'd take Spencer in for a recheck only to find that he still had strep. After the third antibiotic, he finally tested negative. The next day, June 1st, we left town for the wedding in Kansas. By June 6th he had his first seizure. Oh God!

Flashbacks of all the horrific experiences within the last two weeks replayed in my head. *I'm losing my little boy*, I thought. *I'm really losing him.*

Dear God, could you please give me some answers? I don't know what to pray for anymore. Spencer is still here, but is he really? I don't know. It is so hard to watch him suffer. Please help.

26

Angel

June 18, 2000

"Ma'am?" I got up and walked to the door and looked into the hallway. The nurse was racing down the hall in a flurry. "Ma'am, Ma'am!" Finally catching her attention she turned around realizing that I was, in fact, speaking to her.

"Can I help you?" she asked in a hurried tone.

"I have not seen you since this morning and wondered if you could check on a patient. It's been hours."

"I have been downstairs peeling skin off a burn victim for two straight hours," she said, irritated.

"Oh, how horrible, I'm so sorry. I guess it would have been nice if they could have sent a replacement for you while you were urgently needed elsewhere. I need someone in here to help me with my son now and then. His body goes out of control and it gets exhausting trying to keep him from pulling out his IVs or hurting himself. I haven't eaten since last night." I paused, "I was wondering if someone could cover me while I go to the cafeteria to eat?"

With a sharp tone and attitude she replied, "I'm not sure we can do that right now. We are short-staffed today."

The voice in my head forced me to remain calm, but what I wanted to do was throw a magma-burning wrathful temper tantrum from all this insanity. It was followed, however, with the reminder that if you have attitude, they will have more attitude. I said to myself, *Remember Angie, they are the ones caring for your son when you are not here. Keep the peace, win them over with kindness. FIND the kindness.*

"Nurse, I see two dangerous situations here. If I don't eat soon, I may pass out, and then you'd have two patients to tend to. Secondly, if someone is not here to watch my son and he hurts himself, which he is likely to do, that could present a terrible problem for you and the hospital. I would be sincerely grateful if someone came to relieve me as soon as possible."

"I'll see what I can do." She walked away in a huff.

Within minutes a nursing assistant came to my rescue. She was as kind as could be. She was one of those darlings who floated around Children's Hospital passing along her cheer and a listening ear. So many people wanted to help Spencer, but just didn't know how. *I* didn't even know how.

Learning the power of human compassion and empathy that I'd never experienced, was changing my view of the world. While some people were numb to it, others made up for their insensitivity.

I rattled off my name and gave her a brief overview of what happened to Spencer. Just like everyone who heard the story, her eyes dropped, looking down in sadness and disbelief, trying to figure out what to say. Her cheerful perky posture shrunk into a sad, crumpled slump.

"I'm soooo sorry!" she said apologetically. "You must be devastated."

"Yeah, and I'm kinda weary and hungry too," I replied.

The nursing assistant sparked up and said, "Go get something to eat. I'll be fine."

"Let me fill you in on some of the particulars." I looked over to see Spencer snoring lightly. Sleeping for him had been infrequent over the last few weeks. He resembled my old Spencer. Body still, eyes relaxed. He looked so peaceful, such a handsome little boy. I wanted to stay and watch him sleep, but I had just given the nurse a piece of attitude, so I needed to go, now. Nothing would be the same when he awoke. Spencer would be moving with uncontrollable, spasmodic thrusts. Orbiting around people near him, Spence would lie on his back, knees bent pushing his body around with his feet. We called it the pinwheel. And the peace would instantly evaporate. We would guess moment by moment what to do with him.

"The virus is hitting the basal ganglia section of the brain which is causing a severe movement disorder. He flings himself all over the place like a fish on a line, so please stay close. If he starts to have a seizure, beep the nurse right away. I should be back in twenty minutes or so."

"I'll be fine. Take all the time you need," she said with kindness. I could tell that she didn't want me to worry. She may have gathered that I was a protective mother who made sure her son got the best care possible.

"Thank you. I could kiss you. By the way, what is your name?" I asked.

"Angel," she said.

I smiled. "See you in a while Angel." I sped out the door.

27

Masks

June 18, 2000

When I was in a universe away from Spencer, the aloneness brought on unshed tears. It was a sunny, hot June day, so after grabbing a quick bite in the hospital cafeteria I decided to go for a walk and get some fresh Denver air. Ha! I rested on a bench, looking into nothingness. I could really go for a drink right now or have a cigarette or something. What do other people do, anyway?

I jaywalked across the street. Milling around the Mini-Mart embarrassed to do something that I rarely do and then being caught doing it. Nervy! I was watching the door to make sure no one I knew walked in. Why did I feel the need to defend a simple desire to someone I may know?

Masks hide the parts of ourselves we don't want others to see, because we don't like that part of ourselves either. Or maybe they may recognize themselves somewhere in there, I mused, answering my own question. I looked over the booze and then moved on to the counter.

"Can I help you?" asked the long-haired Marilyn Manson look alike behind the counter.

A bit intimidated I said, "I'll have a pack of Merit Ultra Lights and some matches please."

"Why smoke?" Marilyn guffawed. "I mean, what's the purpose if you're not going to smoke real cigarettes like Camels?"

I explained to him my crisis in less than a minute and he said, "Oh, I am so sorry about your son. I hope he does okay." He quickly rung up my purchase and moved on to the next person in line. This was my first of many odd uncomfortable "I don't know what to say" moments concerning Spencer. While some people like to be pulled into drama, most don't.

I walked to the north side of the hospital where there were fewer people and I scoped out a private smoking area behind the bushes. I felt like I was in high school. Sitting on the rocks, I fumbled to get the pack open. My shaky hands reminded me that my nerves were shot. The morning's events gripped my heart again and I inhaled and exhaled long enough to smoke two cigarettes, snuffed out continuously by the wind. I decided I'd better get back upstairs and relieve Angel of her duties. I dug out my cheap drugstore perfume and sprayed my hands and hair. Then I walked back into the hospital smelling like an ashtray covered with spring fresh dryer sheets. I'm not kidding anyone.

"I know God will not give me anything I can't handle. I just wish he didn't trust me so much."

Mother Teresa

28

Lucid Moments

June 20, 2000

It was another hopeful "let's finish the race" kind of day. Despite all of Spencer's crazy actions, a trace of his previous self emerged. By 3 a.m. he was ranting, "ma ma ma ma ma ma," then, "ja ja ja ja ja ja," over and over again. A sweet sadness came to me by hearing my name. It relieved me to know that he still knew who I was and that I was probably in the room with him.

At 9:30 a.m. when he opened his eyes to the world, he was more alert than I'd seen him in a week. His eye contact was good and his eyes were tracking better. He was seeing things at a closer distance and up to eight or ten feet away. We voted on story time together and Spencer seemed to really revel in it. He was calm and focused. Then at 11:25 the physical therapist, Karla, came in and fed Spencer six bites of yogurt. Spencer smiled for her several times. He liked Karla. She was kind, cute, spoke softly, and handled him gently.

At 12:15, Spencer reached out for my face and puckered up for a kiss. *A miracle*, I thought.

Spencer was not able to eat much of anything except pureed food due to the loss of his swallowing reflexes. Liquids were harder to manage as they go down faster and are much easier to choke on. Each time he tried juice from a straw, he would cough and gag, get scared by the reaction, and the liquid would have to be suctioned out. If he aspirated the juice into his lungs, then he could have another problem—pneumonia. He had difficulty managing a straw himself and struggled to close his lips around it to suck. Every little movement was a monumental effort. Consequently, he had not eaten much for days.

The staff kept him hydrated with fluids from an IV. Spencer had bruises and needle pokes all over each arm from blood draws and the intravenous fluids. My "Incredible Hulk" had pulled out six to eight IVs in four days without proper vision or his usual dexterity. So when he was awake, whoever was in the room could not take their eyes off of him for one second! He kept everyone on their toes; he was never going to be an easy patient.

Another neurologist made rounds while the former doctor attended an out-of-town conference. She left the day after his diagnosis, but was updated daily. Dr. Pearson shared Spencer's case at this conference, looking for insight on how to treat him. Somebody out there just might have the answer.

After Spencer had eaten the yogurt, I anticipated that he was on the upswing. Maybe tomorrow he would eat ten bites and be able to drink a soda pop. The alternate doctor decided to put an NG tube down Spencer's nose and into his stomach so that he could be fed formula directly to his stomach, bypassing all the obstructive swallowing mechanisms. Spencer had dwindled down from 46 to 38 pounds, so Russ consoled me that it was the right thing to do and would supply him with a little extra nourishment. We gave the doctor the go-ahead but warned him about his ability to pull everything out. The doctor stared at us blankly. He had not witnessed any of Spencer's lucid or "Hulk" moments.

Spencer was somewhat calm through the afternoon and had fewer episodes of rage. He was even responding to some of my questions with a headshake which I had not seen for several days. Before bed, I was holding him and we were looking at all the pictures and Field Day ribbons taped to the side of his bed. I was explaining what they all were and what they meant while I recounted memories for him to enjoy. He listened intently.

The next day Spencer reached out for my face and puckered up for a kiss. *Lord, thank you for this!* Later, I reminded him of seeing stars through the telescope on our trip to the planetarium. "Stars. Mommy. Why did you? Daddy. No. No. Get out of here," he said, curtly.

In the early evening he ate a few bites of gelatin and said in his disjointed manner, "Mommy. I want to go." When a nurse was trying to change his diaper, he said, "No, don't do that!"

After Dr. Langberger came in to check to see how his NG tube was faring, Spencer, once again, threw himself into untamed commotion. He hated being within earshot of any comments regarding him. Day after day everyone discussed Spencer. I figure he was just as tired of listening as we were talking.

Hmmmm! But this must mean his auditory processing was still good. I posted a note on the door telling all the doctors and nurses that medical issues were to be discussed in the hall.

Spencer seemed to still know everyone who came to visit and was a good judge of character with the new people he met. Though he couldn't tell us, in a matter of minutes, family members could sense who Spencer liked and didn't like.

Just as predicted, before Spencer went to sleep that night, he pulled out his NG tube. The nurse reinserted the tube through the nose, down the esophagus, and into the stomach for the second time. Spencer fought it all the way … and who wouldn't! OUCH.

Tonight I wrote in my journal.

Today Spencer could suck water out of a sponge.
It reminded me of Jesus' burden on the cross.
I knew what Jesus suffered for…all the sins of mankind.
What was Spencer's suffering for?

29

Neon Sign

June 23, 2000

A few weeks before any of this happened, my brave brother Brent came to take care of our kids one weekend while Russ and I were out of town. Having no children of his own, he had played with the boys endlessly. Brent had been a feisty, daring child with a tender heart and Spencer was his carbon copy. After Spencer got all wound up and unrestrained, Brent gave him a light scolding so that he would not do some of that kid mischief again. Unbeknownst to Brent, when Spencer got his feelings hurt he had a habit of hiding. After looking for some time, Brent started to panic and was about to call us before he made one last effort. *Now where would a six-year-old hide?* he asked himself. He went out to the garage and not wanting to miss one square inch, or have to retrace the hunt, he even looked under the cars! And that's precisely where he found him laid out on the oil stained cardboard, ASLEEP!

When I walked into the hospital room that morning, Brent held Spencer and was softly rocking him. Brent had his eyes closed with his arms wrapped tightly around Spencer, humming ever so calmly. I'd heard Brent sing maybe twice in my life. Was he remembering the normal six-year-old nephew he had spent time with just weeks ago? For now, Spencer was moving constantly, looking like he was having one non-stop seizure. He wasn't, but the virus attacking his brain rendered uncontrollable movement. At this moment, Spencer's neck was strained with his head turned to the right, his face distorted with that constant twitching, and his right arm was swinging violently across his chest. His legs were stiff like an unbendable doll. Trying to hold Spencer, Brent was becoming familiar with what it felt like to be his opponent in a wrestling match.

Later Brent would share with me that he thought that something in the garage had poisoned him and, feeling totally guilty, couldn't bear to watch Spencer anymore. I walked him to his car.

"What can I do Ang?" he asked.

"You came and spent time with Spencer. He knows you love him. That is the best thing you can do at this point. Pray...pray hard!" I hurried and gave him a hug good-bye, before either of us broke down.

Brent went back, kissed Spencer good night, and Russ and I took off for home. Since grandma was anchored there, we could rest our minds from more worry.

Being away from the moment-to-moment theatrics, I had some time to reflect on whatever wedged into my thoughts. We were losing the Spencer we knew to severe brain damage. He was nowhere near normal and no longer recoverable. Though his family was cheering for him, he continually got a thumbs down by the doctors. What we saw was not promising and I wondered if he would have to live out his life at this hospital.

I felt dark in my introspection. I just want my old life back. It was an ongoing song internally sung. "That I would be good, even if I got a thumbs down. That I would be good, if I lost my hair and my youth."—A song by one of my artists. I played it over and over, telling myself that no matter how Spencer ended up, I would love him unconditionally.

At the same time, I felt the queer sensation of empowerment to take my rage back to God and demand what I wanted. *Okay, God,* I prayed, *I really need a neon sign telling me or showing me that Spencer is going to be okay. Also, could you please speak to Father Albert right now and tell him that he really needs to find a different vocation, because I called him two days ago to see if he could come to the hospital and pray for Spencer. He hasn't called me back.*

Before I even got that prayer out of my mouth, my cell phone rang. I picked up.

"Angela?" the voice said.

"Yes," I snickered to myself, recognizing Father Albert's voice.

"This is Father Albert and I am calling about your message the other day. Would it be okay to come pray for Spencer tomorrow? I will be going up to Denver to see some of my friends and I thought I'd stop at Children's on the way."

Well I certainly did not want him going out of his way at this point. So I said, "If it is convenient for you, I'd appreciate that. We've had quite the week."

"So I've heard," he said. "I'll be there around 3:00 tomorrow then."

Neon. P-e-r-f-e-c-t-l-y clear, *Thank you God. Thanks for being at my side, and reaching Father Albert, and watching over Spencer.*

The next day I waited for Father Albert until 4:30 and then had to leave for the prayer service that they were having for Spencer at our local church. On my way, I was wondering why Father was at the hospital and not at the prayer service.

I've really got to lower my expectations of people to avoid disappointment. I was miffed. Russ had stayed behind so he would be there when Father Albert showed up. I just needed to make it through this prayer service, then maybe go home and get some sleep. *I'm counting on your glowing neon sign, Lord. I will be watching for it.*

30

Atlas Man

June 21, 2000

I walked over to my van and fumbled through my purse for a smoke. I wasn't supposed to be smoking in the parking garage, but I had just walked my brother to his car and was too fatigued to go to my own private oasis. Several times I had walked past the smoking lounge outside the hospital but I could not bring myself to join the group of pacing nicotine addicts in their hospital gowns. I would watch them exhaling, wondering if they could breathe out all the pain and misery that was happening in their lives. The stress they endured was almost audible by the fervor in which they inhaled and exhaled their smoke. And now…I was feeling the same mounting despair overtake me. As I lit up, I felt it like never before. On the inhale, I envisioned Mr. Atlas man. Upon the exhale, I envisioned the burdening weight fall away.

The situation with Spencer would have enough gravity by itself, but Russ and I had to be strong for each other and the kids. That was our job. On top of that, Russ and I had to be the liaison for those coming to the hospital to see Spencer for the first time. On the outside, both of us wore a strong, knowledgeable medical executive persona. As friends and family members kindly showed up to support us in our crisis, we became increasingly weary.

We appreciated their motives, but when they saw the culmination of shock and devastation that we had experienced in two weeks in just a 30-minute visit, they left overwhelmed and there was nothing we could do for them. With each visitor, we would spend the entire time explaining what had happened to Spencer. We felt it our obligation to inform them, but now we were living the last two weeks over and over again. We couldn't lend any positive news about the state Spencer was in, and that broke everyone's hearts. Watching the sadness on people's faces accompanied by welling tears was a common reaction. Those who remained strong in the hospital room told us later that they wept on the way home.

I let out a big drag of smoke wishing it were something stronger. "Oh, God…please show up." I wailed. Before I knew what had happened, I had collapsed to my knees and started sobbing. My voice echoed through the parking garage, raging in a one-way conversation with God.

"You said you would never leave me or forsake me. Well, I am feeling so alone now and full of fear like never before. You said you would never give me more than I could handle. I am in way over my head and I see no way out. I am very angry about that!"…And then I laughed! I could hear that dumb goofy song I use to sing to the radio. "They're coming to take me away he he, ha ha; to the funny farm where life is beautiful all the time and those men in their long white coats…" I funneled the music into a yowling rant: "What do you want from me, God? What am I suppose to do with this crisis? Help me. Please help me!"

An enveloping peace came over me from my head down. Then God spoke to me. Not in the thunder shaking voice you'd expect, but in this still, small voice in my spirit. He commanded, "Tell your Story, Angela. Tell your story."

That night I added an audio recording as a journal entry. I would be journaling more specifically from now on.

Somehow God would get me there, I knew. A book perhaps? My frantic tears turned to salty relief. I had been bargaining with God to spare my son's life, with the very same God who blessed me with this beautiful child in the first place.

The clouds in my mind and I parted company as I remembered another boy from our community. He suffered from a genetic disease called Spinal Muscular Atrophy. Their strength as a family is a testimony of faith. Their motto is: If God brings you to it, He'll get you through it. In this I found my mojo!

IF GOD BRINGS YOU TO IT,
HE'LL GET YOU THROUGH IT!

31

First Vision

June 24, 2000

The peaceful, comforting drone of praying voices filled my ears. My eyes gazed upon the Eucharist placed on the table on the altar. Our family had been through the worst month of our lives and now I was at my home church with those few friends and family members who mattered most. This prayer service was divined to pour their hearts out to God for Spencer's healing. I felt honored and thankful for the love they gave our family yet was longing for my husband to be beside me. He was still at the hospital with Father Albert. My mother was by my side, holding me dear, and that was a blessing.

This spiritual moment grew more intense as we prayed. I became deaf to the voices around me and my vision was a haze of smoky-white clouds surrounding the Eucharist. I kept my focus on the Eucharist, trying not to come undone. *Concentrate!* I instructed myself. The Eucharist is the unleavened bread that, after consecration, Catholics believe to be the body of Christ. It is the bread and the body received during communion.

The landscape seen through the church windows disappeared. The people around me were no longer in the foreground. The body of Christ—the Eucharist—hung in mid-air on beautiful white clouds. I looked around to see if anyone else might be experiencing the same thing. The rest of the people continued on in their prayerful droning. I clenched my hands tightly together to join them and felt the jab of my wedding ring. I felt an urgent need to look back at the Eucharist and refocus. I took a deep breath allowing the clouds to come back into my periphery. A deep sense of indescribable peace came over me—a peace I am not sure I had ever felt before. Then the Lord showed me His sign.

In the center of the host, I saw a black shadow of a two-month old fetus. It looked like a pollywog. Just like the clouds that floated in, the black shadow of the fetus floated away.

But what does it mean in my life right now, Lord?

A still, small voice rose up in me and said, "Angela, your baby will be fine. Your baby will be fine. Your baby will be fine." NEON.

32

Man of Few Words

June 25, 2000

Resurfacing at the hospital that Sunday morning were my parents teamed with Spencer who had been in ICU the last two days due to the uncontrollable movement and more seizures. Disappointment overcame me as I noticed he wasn't provided with the medical staff's individualized care that we had requested. I selfishly dropped my purse with a loud thud giving no thought to Spencer sleeping.

"It's been over two weeks. Why can't the doctors figure out what's wrong with my guy? When I am not here, I am researching day and night and I think I have a better idea of what's wrong with him than they do." Residual frustration from lack of control came pouring out of my mouth.

My mom's heartache was evident by her expression. She tried to turn her attention back to Spencer, who was awakened by my callous entrance. My dad was sitting in the rocking chair, his face somber and pensive.

"Angela," he said with conviction. I made eye contact. He paused after getting my attention.

"Maybe we are not supposed to know. Did you ever think that maybe God doesn't want us to know all the answers?

That's His job. Think about giving up control, Angela and just focus on taking care of Spencer. Church starts in about a half hour. Maybe a nice walk to the Cathedral would set you right."

And I walked. Ten blocks away from the hospital was The Denver Catholic Cathedral. It gave me some time to sort myself out. Just as my Heavenly Father tried to reassure me the night before with the message "your baby will be fine", my earthly father chimed in with "Let go, let God."

The hour at church was spent trying to give up control I never had in the first place. My father is a man of few words, but when he speaks, the message is often profound. And he was right; the walk was what I needed. My eyes caught the beauty of the stained glass windows. Each one told a story of Christ's walk to the cross. Oh, the trials and suffering my Savior went through were many for a man of 33, I thought. I was 36, and my trials had just begun. If the Savior of the world had to suffer, what makes me think I am exempt?

I started to realize how ridiculous I had been in trying to one-up the doctors with my persistent research . . . as though I knew more than any of them. Really! It occurred to me that my motivation could be that if I had found the source of Spencer's illness, then I would be the hero for my son that I would want to be; love to be.

Seeing the homeless people as I passed them gave me a dose of humility, a reality check that touched my already burdened heart. Equipped with a newly found tolerance, I could not heartlessly assume these people had brought this dire existence upon themselves simply by the choices they'd made in life. Now I wondered what had happened in their lives that would result in their homelessness. Fate? Like us in a way. By no fault of his own, I have a child with a sick brain! You know people always say "count your blessings" and

I'm going to make a pact with myself to do just that, right here and now! I let go of my self-pity and thanked God for all that was good in my life.

> *Hope…rejoice in our suffering.*
> *Suffering produces perseverance*
> *Perseverance—Character.*
> *And Character—Hope.*
>
> Romans 5:3

33

Normalcy

After a few weeks of hospital life, we set up a system for family and friends to take the night and early morning shifts caring for Spencer. Russ and I alternated days during waking hours. Our goal was to have a family member or friend with him around the clock. Nurses Tarin and Rob signed on with Spencer as their patient every shift they had. On Russ' day off he would go to work and on my day off, I'd go home to spend time with Elle and Evan.

Being at home seemed overwhelming too. We had only been in our house ten days when this ordeal began, so there was nothing but boxes to unpack. Our house felt vacant, but waiting to be loved. I would try to do the creative stuff like hang curtains and pictures to get that feeling of home, but we had a long way to go before we could start making memories. Even though it couldn't be helped, I missed Evan and Elle terribly, and felt guilty for being away most of the time. As a stay-at-home mom, I had not been away from my kids much at all. Enjoying the gift of normalcy in the other kids, made me realize how much I had taken them for granted. The kids wondered about my more than usual hugs and constant "I love yous". They got me through each day. I thanked God for their health daily and hoped for some of that to return to Spencer.

My Elle was full of joy and life as always and brought a smile to my face. Evan was quieter than he usually was and seemed to be distancing himself from others. We didn't elaborate about the hospital catastrophes and, in fact, cushioned the kids from the truth until we could understand it ourselves or until the situation improved. When the kids visited, they could only tolerate Spencer for a short time. Seeing him so diminished frightened them, so we spent their visiting time trying to entertain them.

I was missing time with Russ too. All our conversations had to do with Spencer or the care of the other kids. We found solace in the privacy of our room. Embraces intertwined with sorrow can make the world seem okay, at least for a few stolen minutes.

For nine weeks I would set up hospital shifts for the next night, and then call on a handful of volunteers—our beloved family and friends. Then I would pour over hospital records and search as much information as possible. Channeling my thoughts to research pushed me to do more and more. But I was not eating well and was sleeping less. Late at night I could be found on the front porch watching the stars in order to unwind. I'd alternate between tears, praying, and endless God questions. My pillow found me about midnight, and I'd start it all over again first thing every morning, checking on Spencer.

34

A Small World

June 26th, 2000

"Hey Rob, how's it going?" I asked as I walked into the kitchen we all shared on the third floor. He had been in a meeting with all the eating disorder patients, making sure each were consuming their snacks and documenting their intake for the day.

"Not bad, Angie. What's up? I've been feeling lately that I knew you before now... like we've met before this whole Spencer thing. Did you run track in High School? Yeah, we met at a track meet! I asked you out to a Styx Concert and you turned me down. You went to Columbine, right?" he chuckled.

"No way, really?" I laughed out loud. "I think I remember now. Columbine class of '82 and you went to Jefferson, right?" He nodded "We exchanged phone numbers at the track meet and talked on the phone for several weeks."

"Yeah, I think so. What a small world, huh?" he said.

"No kidding! Well, I hope you've forgiven me for turning you down…my mom wouldn't let me date until I was 16."

"Oh sure, nice try. You just didn't want to go out with me," he said.

"No really, I remember. Plus, I was kind of shy with boys," I confessed.

"Oh really? You didn't seem shy. But it's all good. We're both married now."

"Who ever thought we would get reacquainted like this, huh? I am so glad you are Spencer's nurse! He really likes you. It's probably a guy thing and you're the greatest guy in the universe right now!"

"Well that's good. I like Spencer too. He's a great kid with great parents," Rob said.

"Thanks Rob. We're trying our best." I turned around to make a cup of coffee.

"I suppose I'd better get back to work," he said.

"Okay, maybe I'll see ya at the next Styx Concert." I laughed.

Rob laughed as he walked out the door. "I don't even like Styx anymore. Now, Stevie Nicks…well, that's a different story."

Children's Hospital turned out to be a magnet for reunions. I had lived with six nurses my senior year of college in a hundred-year-old house that we were sure had ghosts. There was one teacher and six nurses all studying hard their last year of college to get our GPAs up so our parents wouldn't know how much goofing around we'd done.

When Nurse Melissa walked into Spencer's room one night shift, I had my back to her tending to my boy. When she spoke, I knew she has to be Melissa—one of my old roommates. And when I turned around we immediately recognized each other. Thirteen years later we were both married with children and both tied to Children's Hospital.

The mother of one of the kids in Spencer's class, Lisa, work at Children's on another floor. On break, she would check to see how Spencer was doing and write us kind notes. After Spencer got out of the hospital, I would often see Lisa in the carpool line. She'd always offer to help any way she could.

Two of the kids on fifth floor Oncology belonged to
two mothers I knew. Mary was a friend from my Bible study
in the town from which we had moved. We had prayed
together four years earlier when her daughter was diagnosed
with cancer. Now Laura was eleven and in Children's for her
third time, fighting cancer, confined to her room with zero
immune system. The suffering from her illness had made her
severely depressed.

Some of the oncology "astounding stories" she told
completely threw me for a loop. Yet she told them almost
robotically. I guess she was a more seasoned Children's
Hospital mom. It can be easy to become numb to the crisis
around you. After spending weeks, even months there, it
becomes the norm.

Mary told me about when they found out that Laura
had cancer for the third time. She asked her 11-year-old,
"Are you willing to fight for your life again? If you are not in
it 100%, I understand. But I need to know before we start
with the chemo and bone marrow transplant."

I cried that night for both of our kids. I could not
imagine the reasons behind the suffering they endured.
Mary taught me to remain strong, possess a positive attitude
for your child, and to put your faith in God even when you
don't feel like it. I would hold onto her two scriptures for
years to come.

"I'll refresh tired bodies. I'll restore tired souls."
Jeremiah 31:25

"Rejoice always, pray constantly."
1 Thesselonians 5:16

35

Good-bye Grandma

June 27, 2000

There were nights I would drive to my parents' house as they lived closer and stay over when I had to be back to the hospital the next morning. Sometimes I'd get there late and collapse onto the floor, face down on a carpet of many colors from the 1970s. I've heard that if people, particularly priests, are especially serious about prayer they lay prostrate on the floor and, luckily, I was already there! I prayed for a huge breakthrough, a miracle for Spencer. "Virus please STOP before doing anymore brain damage," I prayed. I woke up an hour later, still face down.

The phone rang at 3 a.m. and I aroused from my fitful slumber. I found the phone but one of my parents had answered and the conversation was already over. Assuming it was the hospital calling, I called them back immediately. When I spoke with the nurse on duty, she reassured me everything was fine, Spencer was asleep, and "no" they did not call. I wondered who called in the middle of the night, but I couldn't keep my eyes open, so I fell back into bed.

When I walked up for breakfast, I became quickly aware of the solemn mood. My parents said, "good morning" but their tone said "sad morning". Once we were all seated, my mom said, "Angela, we have some bad news."

Gulping and grasping, feeling faint and nauseous, I couldn't believe I hadn't been there at the end for Spencer and I wanted the world to just stop!

And slowing down, she continued. "Grandma passed last night in her sleep. It was quick and painless."

I got up from the table, not knowing what to say. Did I hear her right? Always practical and strong in times of crisis, my no-nonsense mother had somberly announced her mother's passing. My heart burst for my mother from a deep reservoir of unwashed misery.

"Oh no, not grandma! Isn't there enough suffering right now? And now this." I wiped my salty eyes.

Mom and her siblings would hold grandmother's funeral over the 4th of July weekend in Kansas. It was then that I realized that I wouldn't be able to leave Spence to attend. One of the biggest celebrations of life ever, and I would miss it. I would have to celebrate her in my heart.

In the hospital room that day, when Spencer was quiet, my grandmother's life and childhood memories came to me: the proper pinkie position required for her tea parties, the holiday decorations she made, and the gathering of family and friends enveloped me with love. Riding down the old wooden stairs on a huge stuffed teddy bear, playing the piano in the music room, taking baths in the old fashioned claw foot tub, playing all day on the tire swing, walking to the creek with cousins, catching rain water off the roof to wash my hair, indulging in her scrumptious bubble bread. Another milestone. God, I would miss Grammy.

A meeting of medical minds was slated for tomorrow to determine if all possible treatments for Spencer had been exhausted, or if there were options yet untapped. As the fear of the meeting began to take root in me, I fought it down with the strength I borrowed from my grandmother.

She filled me and possessed my heart in defense of life—Spencer's chance. I knew the timing of her death tied into my Spencer somehow.

I would not give up searching for a way my son could be healed and neither should they. So I wrote a letter addressed for them.

Letter Read at Care Plan Meeting:

My last joyful memory was on Spencer's 6th birthday while we were at a cousin's wedding. I made my shy second son come out and dance with me. He sheepishly agreed, and we danced and danced and danced. Ever since the seizures enslaved him, he's been in the hospital, however; no one knows with any certainty what's wrong with him.

I don't know what God has in mind—no one does— but I intend to fight for Spencer every step of the journey back to this world . . . and I ask each one of you to continue to do the same. Every time I felt I had no more to give, I gave a little more. Each time I was losing hope, I prayed for strength and courage. I'm begging you to do the same. And if you feel like there is nothing more you can do for Spencer, put your child in his shoes and think again. I will not give up hope until I feel his last breath whisper goodbye.

My grandmother recently passed away at the age of 91. As a young woman she was told— because of the RH factor—that she would not have healthy children. She went on to bear 15 children, have 79 grandchildren and could claim over 100 great-grand-children. She wasn't about to give up. She had more love, strength, and spirituality than anyone I know. She held high standards for herself and those around her and was a continual inspiration to us all.

Thank-you all for everything you have done for us! You have worked so hard and done all that your knowledge has allowed you to do. It has been a long haul and it is not over. I see hope on the horizon.

When I looked up from reading this note, there was not a dry eye in the room. The awkward silence was broken as the meeting ended.

36

IVIG Treatments

June 30, 2000

The care plan meeting was nerve-racking for the two of us being in a room full of doctors, specialists, therapists, residents, and nurses who had all taken time-out of their busy schedules on our behalf; on Spencer's behalf. The fact that every medical treatment had been explored left them feeling defeated as professionals and us helpless as parents. The doctors in the room represented many more as they had taken Spencer's case to conferences in hopes of tapping into some unknown treatment that they had not considered. The finale was an upcoming treatment—a shot in the dark—but they were willing to dive in. We had high hopes that it would stop this unknown virus from ravaging any more of Spencer's brain.

The concurrence at the meeting was to begin as many intravenous immunoglobulin treatments (IVIG) as possible. The blood given to a vein had captured the antibodies that were extracted from over 1,000 blood donors. The transfusions are used to tackle immune deficiencies, inflammatory autoimmune disease, acute infection, and some viral diseases. The Immunoglobulin G (IgG) is a long lasting antibody that maintains control over infections after the body has gone to war with invading bacteria—or in Spencer's case, viruses. The IVIG may do one of three things: provide antibodies the patient lacks, signal the immune system to slow itself down from chronic overdrive, or serve as a decoy to prevent the body from attacking itself.

Spencer received five IVIG treatments over the course of a week. A fever of several days duration disappeared, and Spencer's neurological decline proved to be stable. Much of the severe agitation, screaming, thrashing, constant hand and facial movement subsided after the treatments. Success! Depending on which doctor we talked to, some attributed his improvement to the treatments and others said that the virus was done running its course and he was going to improve despite the treatment or not. Those treatments were so costly, I wanted to believe that they had aided in stopping the virus from causing further brain damage.

37

Dr. Healey, An Angel on Earth

There were many devoted people who helped immeasurably throughout Spencer's ordeal. The kindness of friends and family exemplified compassion. One angel was our pediatrician, Dr. Healey. Each week he requested an accounting of Spencer's progress and, after every conversation, assured me he was praying for us always. On a last minute's notice, he furnished us with prescriptions or provided all the necessary paperwork to enable us to qualify for state funding. And more intimately, he'd listen to a mother's heartache, and he'd feel pain and frustration along with us, give us advice, and allow himself to be accessible any time we needed him! Our Godsend attended to us with grace, humility, and surprisingly, a sense of humor. The last time Dr. Healey had seen Spencer, he was feeling the ill effects of the "Dylantin hangover" as he called it. After that, he had only gotten updated reports via phone or faxes from the hospital. When visiting again after the "meeting of medical minds" to check on Spencer, he was shocked like the rest. As I spoke with another doctor, he sat on Spencer's bed, surrounded by padded walls, and talked to him, rubbing his legs. Dr. Healey began looking around the room, eyeballing a collage of colored pictures, letters from family and friends, a picture of my kids as angels, a quilt made by Spencer's

Vacation Bible School friends, and his Field Day ribbons. When I finished my conversation with another doctor, I turned to apologize to Dr. Healey for making him wait. He shattered us with his own tears.

Swallowing hard he said, "I cannot even begin to imagine what you two have been through this last month. How are Evan and Elle handling this? I am so sorry that I have not been here more for you."

After Dr. Healey left, Russ and I looked at each other, holding back tears, AGAIN. We were realizing that when we weren't dealing with crisis, reality was easing us into the fact that life had changed quickly and would never be the same. Dr. Healey was one of the many angels on our side. We would meet many more who would help us bring balance to our life with Spencer.

38

Dora

July 1, 2000

Everyone had left town for the long 4th of July weekend, including my family. Most of the staff we'd gotten to
know from Children's had the holiday off too. We were
feeling alone in our Spencer world, lacking the energy for
another complete day of the unexpected. I could have used
a movie day with my family to take my mind off everything. I walked up to the third floor nurses' station to get an
update on Spencer. I stumbled upon a nurse monitoring his
peripherally inserted central catheter (or PICC line) that is
used for intravenous delivery of fluids and medicines. The
nurse noticed that the line had infiltrated, a fancy way to
say "infected" and could no longer be used. Immediately,
he was prepped for surgery to remove and replace it with
a BROVIAC type catheter. Just like the PICC line, this
catheter is tunneled under the skin and placed in one of the
veins just under the collarbone.

 I threw my bottle of Gatorade. It whizzed across the
shiny polished floor, abruptly hitting the rocking chair that
Dora was sitting in. She was trying to catch up on paperwork.
Dora was one of my favorite nurses because she had a good

balance of knowledge, sensitivity, and cheer. She was probably around my age and had children of her own. I know God put her there that day to help me manage my outbursts. Like mother; like son!

I returned to the room and saw Dora making busy tidying Spencer's bed. She informed me that Spencer was in good hands and that his daddy was with him in surgery. I sat down in the rocking chair, put my hands to my face and let this hot mess dissolve. Dora sat down on the bed across from me and became still until I could collect myself enough to talk. And then she asked for permission to step out of that "professional mode" into one mother speaking to another. Was it okay with me?

"Yes, of course it is. I wish more people could go here with me," I said. "I know that I'm not alone, but I wish I didn't feel like I am. I miss my family. I miss my grandma!"

Dora told me to pray for the small things, like what I wanted Spencer to do that day, instead of taking in the whole picture and the whole of his problems. We discussed our spiritual beliefs and the importance of prayer and Dora mentioned that she was praying for our family daily. In her, I found another angel at my side! I vented my worries and random thoughts, including the biggest one: how was I going to manage this child the rest of my life? She reminded me to take one day at a time, sometimes second-by-second. She talked about her girls and how difficult it would be for her if this were happening to one of her children. Dora believed that Russ and I made a good team and that we could tackle this thing together.

I asked her, "Why is it so hard for any medical personnel to talk with me like you are right now?"

"Angie, we are taught in medical school to separate ourselves from the emotions of our patients and their families, otherwise we would not be able to stay in this profession very long. There are professional boundaries that have to be established, so that we can do our job properly. Mixing emotions with science is a bad combination." She explained, to my relief.

Then a light dawned on me. I wanted to know how Spencer's illness affected them emotionally, spiritually, and professionally. Much of the stress I stored kept on building day and night. Here, I was sharing so much emotion and they—being professional—were disregarding my emotions and not trading theirs with mine. And, being extremely vulnerable, I felt disregarded. Though a few walls cracked, no one ever broke down. I wanted them to crumble too, to share that and be there with me in my misery.

After Spencer was discharged from the hospital, I sent a letter to many medical staffers that I had gotten to know. In hopes of writing a book, I asked that they would tell me about the emotions they struggled with in the weeks that they cared for Spencer. I was grateful for their written words and pleased that they could be open to it.

Dora's note said that she had a dream about Spencer, Evan, and Elle jumping on the bed. They were singing that "Three Little Monkeys" song. Chucking uncontrollably, one would fall down, knocking the other down, only to get back up and start all over again. She told me she felt like God gave her that dream to hold onto hope that our Spencer would heal. That maybe he would improve enough so he could play with his brother and sister again.

What we had in common was shared hope. Then just as my eyes had dried, she handed me a stuffed animal, a silky soft black monkey. She said, "Here, I wanted to give this to Spencer before he moved up to rehab, but I think this moment is appropriate. When you give it to Spencer, please explain

my dream, okay?" Through hot tears, I took the monkey and
thanked her. Spencer slept with that monkey all through his
hospital stay and years after. I would often sing the "Monkey"
song and tell him that it was from Dora. I instructed him to
get better so he could jump on the bed like a real monkey.
He would smile. I'd like to think he remembered Dora.

39

Smiles and Words

July 1, 2000

Glimmers of hope seemed to surface when we needed them most.

When they brought Spencer up from surgery, he was more alert than I'd seen him in two weeks. We later realized that after anesthesia, Spencer's brain was often more 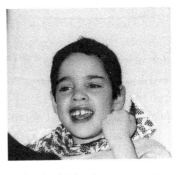 focused and alert than usual. He looked like he was trying to tell me something important. Spencer's facial expressions looked familiar. His facial twitching and tongue movement had stopped due to the remaining amounts of anesthesia. I could not take my eyes off of him. Then he said, "I don't like...I don't like..."

Surprised but wanting to understand, I responded, "You don't like what? Guessing his thought, I said, "The arm restraint?" He nodded yes.

Russ said, "How did you know that?"

"I don't know," I said, "it could be the fact that every time he's restrained, he goes crazy."

We negotiated with Spencer, insisting the catheter remain in place—that he's not to rip them out from under his skin. He realized he was found out and smiled crookedly. Our conversation that day was about the 4th of July weekend with all the beautiful fireworks. He would parrot our words but July came out as "jelly". Russ and I would look at each other and laugh. We were so excited that he was suddenly and sporadically talking. Surprise encouraged us to engage him for more. "Mommy," he stated. We got a glimmer of our boy back for a few minutes. There was a possibility that his brain was healing. We got a taste of the hope we needed so desperately.

Right on his mark, Dr. Johnson waltzed in to check on Spencer and I reminded him of a day in the ER only a few weeks before. "So Dr. Johnson, I kind of remember you saying in the ER when this began that this would all be a bad memory by the 4th of July. I sure wish you would have been right!" I laughed nervously with sadness lying dormant.

"Well if we'd known then what we know now, I certainly would not have said that. I'm sorry things did not turn out better for you," he replied.

I felt only mildly ashamed for throwing a curve ball, but God I hope I hit my target head on! I wanted these words to sting and bruise his cavalier approach. The raw truth is that parents trust doctors and what they say. Every time they trumpeted some absurd outcome, it was at the expense of our son and us. They left us surfing tidal waves between Spencer's perilous undertow and some unreachable fantasy. At the end of the day, they retreated to their yachts . . . while we clung to a buoy in an endless ocean . . . unable to swim.

"Children's is a bit deserted this weekend, huh? I'm feeling a bit uneasy about leaving him tonight. We've been covering all the shifts because my family is out of town, but Russ and I desperately need sleep tonight. Could you get a CNA (Certified Nurse's Assistant) assigned to Spencer until we return in the morning? I don't feel comfortable leaving him by himself at night. We had talked about a fulltime CNA for Spencer at the care meeting and I was suggesting it again in hopes that they were working on it. *Throw me that life preserver—NOW—won't you?*

I just wanted a night of unworried sleep, floating on the waves of unconsciousness, with no storms to fight.

"Yeah, it's pretty quiet this weekend. I'll see how the plans are coming for the CNA. We can give him sleepy meds to calm the agitation, but it looks like they have only a temporary effect on him. We'll get someone in here so you two can go home. Let's hope the virus is close to running its course and these neurological behaviors start diminishing," he said.

"Amen to that. I want this to be over so we can go home." I sighed.

"I'm with ya on that," Dr. Johnson agreed. "At least we got some smiles and words today. I can be grateful for that." He smiled.

40

My Diagnosis

Meanwhile, Spencer's test results came back! These tests were conducted over the course of several weeks at Denver Children's, the Mayo Clinic, Stanford, and The Center for Disease Control. Listed was every possibility responsible for a life in hell. It was as if the clouds were parting and the thunder was ceasing and we could spot land through a spyglass.

I had researched every single sign and symptom from the onset of this ordeal. No matter what I'd discover, I got no answers and found myself still drowning. I tried to strangle my need to know, and silence the "why us?" "why him?" as the damage was done. I was wasting energy on something I had no control over and could not change. But this—now this—was right here. Now I could know what thief stole Spencer's childhood—one that would be forever changed. The finale of 900 pages of medical records read:

Negative cultures from spinal fluid, blood, and urine samples:

Enterovirus, Herpes 1 and 2, CMV, Mycoplasm, Arbovirus (mosquito or other blood sucking animals), Varicella (chicken Pox), EBV, Human Herpes Virus

6, Bacterial viruses, Brucella, Lyme disease (tic), Bartonella (cat scratch fever), Tuberculosis, RPR, VZV, Ab reactive, St. Lois, Lacrosse Western Equine, Eastern Equine encephalitis, Asian flu, Hepatitis, Myelin basic protein, Sillenium, Lead, Thallium levels, Syndenham's Chorea, SSPE.

For some reason, I believed that whatever got into Spencer's brain was related to his strep infection. Syndenham's Chorea fit my diagnosis. Since Spencer had just had strep and the characteristics of the disease described his behaviors so well, I was sure that is what he had. Even though he tested negative for it, I was convinced that they missed it somewhere along the way. The prognosis that the child recovers 2-6 months after the initial insult is what kept me on this diagnosis for two weeks.

Syndenham's Chorea is a disease characterized by rapid uncoordinated jerking movements primarily affecting the face, feet, and hands. It results from a childhood infection with group A Strep, usually occurring six months after the infection, but not always. Since Spencer had several bouts of strep and the characteristics of this disease mirrored his behaviors, I was sure this was it exactly. However, he tested negative for it.

The symptoms of Syndenham's Chorea are these:

Involuntary movement of limbs, face, torso
Hypotonic (muscle weakness)
Clumsiness
Restlessness
Face grimacing
Poor coordination

Facial spasms
Shoulder spasms
Hip spasms
Onset of symptoms gradual or sudden
Purposeless movements
Irregular movements
Short lasting movements
Choreiform (choppy) movements
Anxiety
Irritability
Weak hand grasp
Smirking facial expressions
Voice changes
Speaking difficulty
Emotional instability
Psychological changes

Stubbornly, I held onto this prognosis because the infected child gets better 2-6 months after the initial insult. It was a better outcome than that for a child with encephalitis, which I was stalling in accepting as a diagnosis anyway. In conversations with God, I found myself wishing FOR this disease, not that one. Wading in the deep end, I always found myself in the very same situation: anchorless.

41

He's Back!

July 9, 2000

About a week after the series of IVIG infusions, Spencer had two phenomenal days of activity. We were positive our Spencer was on the road to recovery. The day began with Spencer sleeping in. When he woke at 11:30 a.m. I gave him a massage to relieve his sore, unruly muscles.

The nurse came in and put Vaseline on Spencer's lips and he sat straight up in bed and said, "I need to p..." three times in a row then lay back down. We assumed that he needed to pee, but when we helped him with the urinal he did not go. After no strength for posturing his body for weeks, Spencer amazed us with the ability and physical control to sit up all by himself. A miracle!

Spencer drank apple juice out of a straw, asked for Mama, gave Grandma a big hug, and sat up by himself throughout the day. When we took a walk around the hall he was grabbing at things in reach. He peed and pooped in the potty, and rubbed his forehead on purpose. When asked if he had a headache, he nodded at us in understanding. I was realizing that he probably had a severe headache this whole time, poor guy. He also told one of the nurses "I'm hot."

All these purposeful words and movements thrilled us. Maybe the virus was done running its course and we were sailing into the bay. A beach house vacation sounded nice about now!

When the doctor arrived to check his IV site, Spencer said, "Who are you?"

"I'm Dr. Susan. And who are you?" she asked.

"Spencer," he said.

When she asked if he was six years old, he nodded. This again was a big accomplishment. Doctor Susan changed the dressing on his BROVIAC. With determination, he lifted his shirt so she could work on it. Usually it took three of us to hold him down during such a procedure, because his movement disorder kept him constantly in motion. Yet he deliberately lay still while she cleaned it and applied a new bandage. I could see that he was concentrating as hard as he could to get his body to lay still.

Grandma rocked Spencer later on, and he looked comfortable, actually comfortable in his own skin. He was snuggling and sitting still without agitation. When she tried to put him in bed for the night, he clung to her and hugged her tight. I felt blessed to have witnessed this (and capture it on videotape as well). It left my Mom pretty emotional . . . surly she felt the blessing too.

Spencer chatted up a storm with the nurse and CNA, Ariana and Brie. When they were talking about the zoo, Brie mentioned snakes and Spencer repeated, "Snakes." Brie thought he must have thought snakes were cool to get such a response. When asked what his last name was Spencer very audibly said, "McCombs." Spencer's limited speech had had an intoxicated slur for over a month now, but this time it came out crystal clear. When the ladies were talking about a popular female singer and how their daughter liked her they asked, "Spencer, do you like her?"

And he abruptly said, "NO!"

Just as Brie was finishing her shift, Spencer called out "Ariana" to keep her with him longer. Brie exclaimed, "Keep him talking!" then looked past her. "See ya tomorrow Spence."

Mom and I went home so bubbly; so buoyed up. It was good to see him talking. We prayed that his improvements would continue and that this was not just a one-time deal. The doctors would tell us that this is common with brain injuries. One minute they're with you and the next minute they aren't. The brain is such an amazing and complex organ and unbelievably mysterious. There is still so much that the doctors don't know about it. We would hear more and more incredible stories of healing brains and other people's recoveries. One thing I learned is if you get sick...you don't want it to be your brain. Everything else seems easier to fix and is more likely to heal.

42

A Walk Down the Hall

July 10, 2000

Spencer had a visit by his Kindergarten teacher, Mrs. Barton. She had the same shocked reaction when she saw how much he'd changed since graduation a month earlier. He looked awfully sick. The sight of him with his skinny, pale, and unworldly appearance was enough of an eyeful, but then to witness an uncharted mind was asking too much. The nurses said that Mrs. Barton talked with Spencer until he got a little agitated, but then he also seemed upset when she left. Spencer loved Mrs. Barton and she loved him.

Mrs. Barton left to go see another student, Carrie on the oncology floor. Carrie's mom and I would meet in the hall now and then to share our stories and support one another. It helped to know that there was someone there at the hospital who understood what we were going through.

When Spencer had his bath this morning, he insisted on standing in the tub. Standing! This was odd because whenever we'd try to get him to stand he would lift his legs up like it was painful. So Tarin washed him standing in the tub. It must have tired Spencer out, since he fell right to sleep upon returning to the room. Tarin removed his NG tube and replaced it when he awoke. He threw a major temper tantrum. It was good to see him fighting back again, intentionally. *Keep up the fight, soldier*, I prayed.

The Physical Therapist, KJ, came to work with Spencer. He gave all he had, but after therapy he got cranky. The endless weeks of fussing were exasperating for him. KJ had him sit, stand, sit, stand, sit, stand. His legs were weak, but he had practiced in the bathtub and he was able to do it for several minutes.

KJ said, "Great job Spencer!"

Spencer said, "I know."

When she asked if he wanted to do it again he said, "NO!"

Spencer went from a very active, athletic six-year-old to the functioning level of a six-month-old.

Dora came in to read to Spencer after therapy about the time he was ready to relax. When Dora began to read, Spencer said, "Don't like." So Dora moved on to where she was needed and Spencer took a much-needed nap.

While Spencer slept, Russ and I usually had to meet with doctors. We took advantage of the time he could not hear us talk. On this day the infectious disease specialist was giving us the results from the CDC and the Mayo Clinic. A couple weeks prior, it was suspected that Spencer had SSPE (subacute sclerosing panencephalitis). This is a disease of the brain caused by the dormant measles, later manifesting into a fatal disorder. Spencer's levels were indicative of this but were found inconclusive because some of his spinal fluid had been tainted at the lab. Did they spill it? Get it mixed up with someone else's? Or did it simply never make it there? So another spinal tap was done and resent for clearer results. This whole waiting process was a month!

Then we got word that Spencer did not have SSPE. Thank God!

Spencer had just woke up when the Occupational Therapist came in the late afternoon. "Busy day, right?" Brian greeted.

Spencer reached over and grabbed the oxygen mask, pulled it to himself and said, "This is mine." Then he told Brian to "move." Feisty at that!

While Brian worked with Spencer, we got the G-tube and Metaport surgery set up with the GI doctor. The Metaport is a device under the skin that would let us administer all his meds directly into the bloodstream. It was more permanent and would soon replace the BROVIAC. The G-tube would allow Spencer to eat all his food through a button-like tube that went directly into his stomach. He wouldn't have to swallow anything, as his brain was still not allowing him to consistently swallow. Spencer would get 12-16 oz. of formula every three hours, plus water to fatten him up! Tubes! Tubes! Tubes! To think that Spencer's life could have been lost to starvation in a previous pre-plastic era.

With all these medical terms and knowledge under our belts, Russ and I kept getting teased that we had our honorary MD degrees. I was beginning to feel like I'd learned as much in a month as I had in my four years of college. And we were paying a hundred times more for it in medical bills! Thank God for insurance or the rest of our lives would be spent in poverty. When it was all said and done we called Spencer the "Million Dollar Man".

Tarin came in and removed Spencer's BROVIAC and he was so happy. Russ asked him if he would like to take a walk down the hall and Spencer nodded. So Russ got him right out of bed and sang the "Put One Foot in Front of the Other" song from Rudolph, and that is exactly what Spencer did. His face was all scrunched up like those quirky little guys in the Wizard of Oz. His feet were moving and he seemed to move them as if to imitate their waddle-walk. We were elated because he was giving it all he had and concentrating so hard. Russ was aiding him by holding his left elbow and hand. When Spencer walked by the nurses' station, they all looked up and started clapping. This made him walk faster. I looked over and saw everyone with tears in their eyes… doctors, nurses, residents. I had never seen that many people at the desk at once. We were all so amazed! By the looks of Spencer five days ago, no one would have expected this. I ran as fast as I could to my car to get the video camera and videotaped another two trips up and down the hall. Everyone was so excited that we finally had a good day with Spencer McCombs to brag about.

Back in the room Spencer continued with a conversation. He was sitting up in his bed leaning against the wall. He looked around and asked, "Where's Evan?" I am sure he was missing his brother terribly. I told him Evan was at grandma's house. He said, "Oh." Then he said, "Mommy?"

"Yes, Spencer?"

"Your Buggy." He was repeating a sentiment that I'd say often.

"Yes, you are my Buggy," I said holding back tears of joy.

I talked about getting barn cats when he got home from the hospital and he said, "Kitty cats" multiple times. He liked hearing himself talk. It must be so unfamiliar to him! Then Russ told him he needed to get better so he could eat his favorite chocolate muffins again.

He said, "Mmmmmm." Smacking his lips, he mused, "Muffin."

"You'd have to brush your teeth after that." I said.

He repeated, "Brush my teeth."

Spencer was holding his white stuffed polar bear named Berit. He started shaking it back and forth. Russ asked, "Who's that Spencer? Who are you shaking?"

"Beeerit," he said.

"Do you love Berit?" Spencer nodded and gave Berit a bear hug.

The resident, Dr. Simon and my friend Kris were so pleased they got to witness this conversation. Spencer was actually Dr. Simon's very first patient, as she was fresh out of med school. She confessed that she went into pediatric medicine because kids get better. On Spencer's bad days, she'd sink along with him.

There seemed to be an unusual amount of activity in Spencer's room this day and I later understood that people were hearing of his improvements and wanted to come check it out themselves.

We were singing praises to God that night, praying that all this would last and that Spencer's abilities would improve from this day forward. It was hopeful to think that if his physical and speech abilities went uphill from today, it would be no time before Spencer was totally healed and on his merry way through childhood. It was awesome to be able to share the videos we'd taken and stories of the day with family and friends. Our first day of good news since it all began. Hope was on the horizon! Milestones!

43

Up to Rehab

July 17, 2000

The day Spencer moved up to the fifth floor was bittersweet. We would miss all the staff that had helped us through the hardest month of our lives, but transferring to rehab meant Spencer was going to get better. The goal was to work with him every day as much as his little body would allow to regain all that he'd lost. Spencer spent a month plus two days in rehab mostly catching up on sleep he'd lost in June.

Since the virus was done running its course, much of Spencer's movement disorder subsided. The doctor was weaning him off the drug Artane, which helped manage his debilitating Parkinson-type movements. He was also being taken off the Dylantin, since his EEG was normal and showed no seizure activity. These were all signs of improvement. With Spencer off of all the drugs, we could truly see what there was to work with. Since there was no evidence of a virus in Spencer's body, encephalopathy, meaning global damage to the brain, was a more general description the doctors were using now. The plain truth is that he had global brain damage on a cellular level. CAT scans showed that his brain had shrunk, leaving larger ventricles. Simplified even more, every area of Spencer's brain was affected by the insult, except maybe his brain stem.

Every morning Spencer would be taken down to Physical Therapy (PT), Occupational Therapy (OT), and on to the speech therapist. He was frequently sleepy and did not do a whole lot. When he was awake, the speech therapist would work with tastes of extracts in suckers in his mouth to wake up his taste buds for eating. Amazingly, he did not like it at all and would gag and drool. Spencer had developed a severe gag reflex that was activated anytime anyone got near his mouth.

The physical therapist would bounce and stretch Spencer on an exercise ball to help redevelop posturing muscles in the back and stomach. His body was a combination of Jell-o and dead weight when picked up. The PT would also help him walk while supported. Many times Spencer would lift his legs because he didn't want to walk. He didn't say it was painful or too much work, but it appeared that his brain prohibited him from standing any length of time. His favorite activity by far was to ride the big tricycle around the halls. The bike ride—a six-year-old activity—usually made him laugh and smile at the world.

The OT therapists would introduce different textures for Spencer to touch with his hands. He was neurologically much like a newborn—very raw, always clenched and sensitive to touch. They taught his unskilled hands to grasp for toys and use other fine motor skills. He startled easily over quick movement or loud noises. Spencer's progress was much slower than I had expected, but the doctors reminded me that his body had been through a lot and he was recovering from the initial insult to the brain.

When Spencer wasn't sleeping or doing therapy, he would enjoy calming music, being read to, or walks in his wheelchair under warm blue summer skies. He would only say one or two words at a time, but that was better than none. But the verbal responses were only by way of direct responses to questions asked—not by any conversation he initiated. He'd blurt out: "Yeah! Out. What did you do? Sure. Happy Birthday. No. Mommy. No fair! Why? Where? Oh. Evan. Stop it. Two. Shut up. Go." and they were the limits to his talk.

I spent much of my days in rehab reviewing the last month's notes, asking questions, and doing more research on brain damage rather than finding what caused it. I would often feel an underground alarm sound as I began trying to grasp the possibility of my child now being defined as "special needs" and how that would change all our lives. An unreachable fear would subside, and then I'd find myself wondering if Spencer could fully recover.

Russ had hope of a complete recovery, since raising a "special needs" child was simply not in his plan. Spencer's rehab doctor, Dr. Worlton, was wheelchair-bound resulting from a car accident she'd had in her twenties. Despite being a paraplegic, she had risen to greatness on her own merits. She possessed a down-to-earth personality with the intelligence belonging to a Ph.D., and yet never addressed us with condescension. She was one of the only doctors who welcomed my every question, asked for more, and was not afraid to say, "I don't know."

On one day that dragged on aimlessly, Dr. Worlton could tell that my hope was faltering. I was figuring that it must have been a one-time deal when Spencer's brain turned on momentarily for one last hurrah and he would not be getting any better. The memory of his walk down the hall played in my mind endlessly. Dr. Worlton sat in the hospital room for an hour and shared stories of several encephalitis patients that she worked with over the years. Many of them had symptoms and behaviors like Spencer's and had recovered almost fully. She told me of a boy who was worse than Spencer. He'd moved away after being released from the hospital. Two years later he walked up to Dr. Worlton and shook her hand. He was able to talk and introduce himself. She didn't even recognize him and was amazed at his recovery. With renewed vision, I chose to keep my sights on that goal for Spencer.

44

Emergency

August 10, 2000

One evening I decided to take Spencer into the bathroom that was available for all fifth floor rehab patients. He might appreciate a calming bath to sleep soundly. The nurses were all busy managing their charges, so why not provide the bath all by myself? In my t-shirt and shorts, I climbed in and sat behind him. I propped him up with my arm extended around him and tried to wash him at the same time. This was not easy unless you were an octopus! By the time we got out of the tub, both of us were spent. A worry intruded on this fatigue . . . curious to know whether I would be capable or unable to care for my child once I was home.

I steadied myself to lift Spencer out of the tub, so my wet feet would not send me skating across the floor. Just as I lifted him out, grabbed the towel with my teeth, dropped it on top of him, he let loose. He was pooping everywhere, just oozing right out of him. "Soooooo much for the bath!" I said aloud.

When I walked across the bathroom to yell for help, I began sliding in the trail he'd left behind. Trying desperately not to drop Spencer, I somehow got the door cracked and yelled, "HELP! Emergency! Someone help, please. I'm in the bathroom!" Then I looked down at my wet shorts, naked shivering Spencer, and the brown splotches dotting the floor. All I could do is burst into laughter. Sometimes it's easier to laugh.

When the nurse ran in she said abruptly, "Oh, you scared me. I thought it was a real emergency!" which sent me into gales of laughter!

"Uh, if I drop Spencer now, it'll cause more brain injury and probably an infection from all this." I said, coughing from the pungent odor.

"You know…like life or death emergency," she said.

"Oh, okay. I get it." I laughed harder.

We bathed Spencer again and got him tucked into bed. It went much smoother with two people. I let the nurse clean up the poop, being the good sport she was, and since this wasn't anything like a life or death emergency and all. The nurse reminded me to ask for help next time and most certainly use a bath chair. , I thought. After the drama, Spencer fell asleep almost immediately. I kissed him and prayed over him, then left for a good night's sleep at home in my own bed.

45

Coming Home

August 19, 2000

The doctors were ready to release Spencer from the hospital and I sat in my family room flooded with worry over the unknown. I had no idea how I was going to take care of this significantly handicapped child plus two other children, but God would show us the way.

The phone rang and it was Spencer's kindergarten teacher, Mrs. Barton, calling. She told me that one of the other hospitalized children, Carrie, had passed away the  night before. With recurring fungal infections, a low immune system, and her little weak body, she couldn't hold on. I hung up, collapsed to the floor and began wailing. Two months of grief dripped onto the kitchen floor. My heart broke for

Carrie's family and mine. How ironic that Spencer was the one who was not suppose to make it, while Carrie was always expected to get better.

The hospital staff had Spencer's room packed up and ready to go so we could hit the ground running. We went to the last care plan meeting with all the doctors present, notebook in hand. Much of the time was spent telling us how to work with the insurance company to get Spencer services once we left the hospital. They had already set up a series of PT and OT appointments, followed by several speech therapies. They directed us to the best way to get a wheelchair. Our formula and feeding supplies were on order. We had already acquired a suction machine and had stocked up on diapers and wipes. We also set up a temporary bed on the floor of our bedroom. All we had to do is get some backup seizure medicine in case Spencer started to have seizures once we got him home.

In the two weeks prior to Spencer's discharge, the nurses and doctors had provided us with the training required for Spencer's care, by letting me do most of it—hands on—with a well-practiced nurse. I would now be spending every moment of my day caring only for him. Two months earlier, I had rushed a six-year-old to the hospital and I now was about to walk out with a 40 pound infant. If only Spencer's re-entry in this world would progress as rapidly as a baby's does. That was our hope and we would do everything in our power to help him.

My mom and dad came to help us with the move and took Spencer outside to the courtyard to wait. Russ and I were in the pharmacy getting Spencer's scripts filled. When we were armed with every defensive medicine science had to offer, we loaded the car then met in the courtyard to get Spencer, our cargo. Grandma pushed him to the big automatic sets of doors when he was spotted. Everyone waved and encouraged us as we wheeled onward. We stopped briefly to thank a doctor who came to say good-bye. Spencer knew he was finally going HOME, and with all the excitement and energy building, he lifted his arm and waved us through the door commanding, "COME ON."

This was his first word and purposeful movement in a month.

The doctor said, "Well I guess you're ready to go Mr. Spencer . . . so I'll let you go, big guy."

As we wheeled him out to the parking lot, my heart beat wildly. I had never been so unprepared for anything in my life. The depth of responsibility I felt for my child's life left me flabbergasted. We got him a brand spanking new car seat so that his gelatinous body would be held together, and promptly buckled him in. Grandma and Grandpa kissed him goodbye and I hugged my mom, extracting as much love and wisdom as I could envision, never wanting to let go. A slow but persistent icy panic was easing its way into my veins as I contemplated this enormous responsibility before me. *How would Evan and Elle react to their "new" brother*, I wondered, *and would they feel the same fear?* We should be as optimistic as possible about Spencer's potential recovery, but the only way I could show this was by wearing a wholly artificial façade. I summoned mercy and grace to guide me, but the truth is that we were happy enough to be back together as family. Together we would love and learn along the way.

When we got home Grandma Jan was there to greet us with a stuffed animal for Spencer. Russ got Spencer out of his car seat, which was of great interest to Evan and Elle. He held Spencer under the arms and he walked up to the house. Surprisingly, Russ got Spencer's legs moving by singing the "One Foot in Front of the Other" song again. As Spencer was boosted on to walk as much as possible to the front door, his facial expression showed tremendous determination to get there. All eyes upon him, and he made it to another finish line! Evan, Elle, and I cheered for him.

When we got him tucked into his bed, the kids came in and I explained his tube feeding apparatus as I was hooking it up. Evan was stunned and listening. All Elle wanted to do was be a little nurse. She put some plastic gloves on, grabbed the suction to the suction machine and said, "Spencer needs suction." We all laughed and Spencer smiled. When we weren't watching, Evan reached over and laid his hand on

Spencer's chest. Spencer reached up and grasped his brother's hand. That was our special miracle for the day.

We sat and talked around Spencer until he dozed off, then spent some time answering questions until bedtime. Seeing that Spencer was grateful to be home, made whatever was to follow next—in terms of care—easier to cope with on my end. Whew! He just wanted to be in his own home and with family. Despite his brain injury, he still knew everyone and loved us just the same. Now maybe he could finally get some sleep without hourly poking and prodding.

Our prayer was short that evening as everyone's emotions were teetering on the brim.

"Lord, we thank you that Spencer is finally home with his family again. We pray for good sleep, continued healing, and love all around. Amen."

PART IV

BARELY ABOVE WATER

"Sometimes you don't realize you're drowning when you're trying to be everyone else's anchor."

-unknown-

46

Grief

2000-2001

"Lord God: help my child who is not whole. Why does my precious one have to suffer every day? Why did my once normal child end up with all these deficiencies? Sometimes I blame myself, sometimes I blame you, and sometimes I just cry. My heart aches, longing for things to be better. I wish I could understand. I love 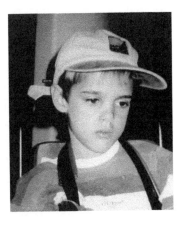 Spencer so much. I value the lessons he has taught us, the strength he has brought to our family that I never knew we had. To me, he is an angel. Grant me patience—daily—yet give me determination, perseverance, and consistency to make his life, and all our lives, more fulfilling, more purposeful. Give me wisdom and sensitivity to hear your voice when I am not able to hear his. Help me to be realistic in my expectations of him, my other children and in my husband

and myself. Grant me strength when I am weary and weak; a calm spirit when I am frustrated. Remind me to praise even small accomplishments to help build self-esteem, even when I feel like I have nothing left to give. Let me cherish each day we are blessed with. Let us learn from every experience and pass it on so that others may receive what we are giving. Thank you Lord for Spencer and remind me that in your eyes, he is whole. Until he dances in heaven… Amen."

Praying with Spencer is a supernatural experience. It's as if his brain tunes in during prayer. And so, we pray a lot. I pray with him, even when my anger at God leaves me void of prayer elsewhere.

In the first two months of being home, Spencer could not make any eye contact because he was temporarily blind. His eyes were open, but it looked like he was staring into a non-existent horizon of another world. It was due to brain cells that were still dying off. The day I prayed this prayer with him, however, he crawled out of that black hole like he actually saw me and not just heard me. I stared into his eyes and I watched them come into focus. With flickers of hope, and squinting back tears, I said, "Welcome back Spencer. You can see me, can't you?" His breathing quickened with excitement and a slight smile appeared. And then the moment was gone.

These moments came more frequently over the next year, until his vision was mostly restored.

Caring for Spencer throughout the first year meant integrating schedules for our one special needs child with one busy athletic brother and his girly-girl sister. Mix that with maintaining a marriage between two overwhelmed parents and then stir that up with our other family members. If that isn't enough, then you add one heaping side of operating a thriving family business, and that's the whole pie. Since

Russ inherited a lead role in his family's business, he'd have to work extra hours but could also take off personal time for a whirlwind of appointments.

Elle was three, in pre-school and loving it. Her joy was in helping Momma around the house. On her own, she could be found playing horsey, and caring for all our animals. She enjoyed ballet classes, but Elle was all about animals! Evan was entering third grade and having a hard time adjusting to his "new" brother. He had high hopes for the return of his beloved Spencer, but the loss of his best friend devastated him. He attended counseling sessions to release all his stored heartbreak. He developed a friendship with his new bestie who helped with this difficult transition. Involvement in Boy Scouts allowed him more time with his father and they both loved that. Russ and I had to find our way back to each other, as a couple, and we found it with weekly date nights.

The doctors informed us that what we were able to recover in this single year with Spencer, as far as recapturing any previous ability, was probably what he would have for the rest of his life. This meant that everything we could do to bring him back would depend on our capabilities too. A light came on. It then became obvious that he'd get far more benefit from some kind of structured home plan, a one-on-one calculated play, than by letting him swim among all the other fishes at school. He'd drown.

Spencer's days were again filled with multiple therapies, teacher's visits, and taking part in family activities. This home re-entry appeared to be beneficial for him while he was getting stronger and learning. With an insult to the brain, it typically takes up to three months to see improvement. There was no magic formula for recovery, but the doctors were giving us something to grasp onto. From three to six months, the recovery should speed up, then from six months to a year even more rapidly. That was the goal.

We saw tiny improvements with posturing and eye contact, and we watched his awkward movement disorder vanish. He gained some intentional movement with his arms, but only marginally so. Overall, progress was s-l-o-w. Day after day, we'd hear of stories of encephalitis and meningitis recoveries that delivered hope. Acting on it, I scoured the Internet for a Spencer pen pal. Week by week we expected more, naturally, but we saw little progress. By summer's end, it was clear that we may be living with a severe needs child for the rest of our days. Russ was not giving up; he believed wholeheartedly that Spencer would recover fully.

Once we exceeded therapies through our insurance carrier, we returned to research what we could do on our own. My mother and sister helped me several days a week so that I could spend time with Evan and Elle. A friend from church arranged for dinners to be delivered for almost a year. Bless her and the many varieties of lasagna from Castle Rock, Colorado! When I had an errand or activity outside the house, it was a welcome break from his care—a life preserver. My life was completely consumed by Spencer, and I was sleeping, on average, four hours a night. *Is either one of us getting better?* I wondered.

There were days when Russ and I would look around the house, wondering where the day went. There didn't seem to be any proof of anything done! One part of raising a special needs child is the 24/7 care of their immediate needs. Another part, though, is the mound of paperwork and phone calls to be sure they are getting the funding and supplies to hold it all together. Added to this balancing act, it was equally important to get involved with a support group of other parents who already learned how to tough it out. They offered advice for managing e-v-e-r-y-t-h-i-n-g forever.

With a hot mug of coffee in hand, I recharged my spirits by reading one of the support group newsletters:

> "Did you ever sit down after an exhausting day, look around, and see a messy house and you ask yourself, 'What in the world did I do all day?' Or better yet, your spouse gets home from work and asks the same question. You never took a break, yet you seemed to accomplish nothing all day. Next time you feel this way, check the list and see which ones apply to you!

Calls to make:
- Schedule doctor's appointments
- Schedule home health care services
- Call physical therapist about getting new wheelchair
- Order new wheelchair
- Make appt. for wheelchair insert fitting
- Call insurance about coverage
- Make appt. with orthopedic surgeon
- Call pharmacy for prescriptions
- Call in diaper order
- Set up respite care
- Make therapy appts.
- Call social services about reimbursement forms
- Call social security office about income changes
- Call special education director about school problems
- Call teacher about IEP changes
- Call advocate to come to IEP meeting
- Call teacher about observing child in classroom
- Call parent advocacy group for classes

- Call dentists in town to see who takes Medicaid
- Call hospital about mistake on billing
- Make an appt to check blood levels
- Schedule another EEG
- Call school bus not to pick up child
- Call neurologist to tell about odd seizure
- Set up orthotics appt.
- Call around looking for a van to buy
- Call babysitter for other children's appts.

Things to Do:
- Search internet for information
- Do range of motion
- Do speech therapy exercises
- Observe child at school
- Meet with advocate
- Attend IEP
- Train new respite provider
- Look for ongoing qualified respite providers
- Write letter to dept. of education
- Take child to doctor appt.
- Go for communication evaluation
- Write letter appealing to insurance company for more therapies
- Pick out wheelchair
- Look at vans
- Take van in for lift installation
- Go to hippo therapy
- Go to social security for SSI evaluation
- Pick up forms at social services
- Pick up prescriptions
- Fill out waiver forms
- Attend support group meeting

- Take child in for blood levels
- Check emails
- Plan date night
- Take a shower (?)
- Take other kids to sporting events, tutoring, church events"

The list seemed endless as it was in our home . . . our work was never done. I knew I was no longer able to keep up the pace as Spencer's main caregiver, as I was running out of gas. Russ started taking the night time hours, while working a fulltime job. We hired a caregiver, really—an angel. Nicole arrived. Hallelujah!!

47

NACD

Sitting against our motor-home somewhere in southern Colorado, we could see Spencer wheeled up to face a big beautiful sky, and we were all smiles. It was a delightful, sunny, summer day on our way to Utah.

"Spencer, you got some big teeth coming in there. You need to learn how to eat again so you can use those puppies. Huh, buddy?"

Spencer responded by laughing uncontrollably like he was being tickled from the inside out. His huge new front teeth took over his face, making all of us crack up watching him. Silly goofball! It was exciting to see him happy; his joyful moments were pretty rare. Everyone exhaled in relief. His brain was currently waking up to episodes of hysterical laughter, building higher and higher and more uncontrollable until it was abruptly halted by attacks of coughing. Crazy! We never knew what he was laughing at, if anything. But whenever we would talk, he would laugh harder and louder.

"Hey my little man, Dr. Daman, therapist at large, is going to give you some new exercises so we can get you eating again," I said. Spencer gave us squeals of laughter.

Russ walked out of the camper, "What's so funny, big guy? You being a silly, funny, goofy kid? Whataya think . . . can you take over driving tomorrow? I bet you'd have fun driving the motorhome." More laughter hit the sky.

Sparring between Spencer and the rest of us went on for about twenty minutes until a coughing attack required suctioning. All hands on deck! After that he was depleted of any razzmatazz; he dozed off for an afternoon nap. It was times like this that we lived for. These were moments where we knew Spencer was not feeling pain or suffering in any way and it carried us a long way to reconcile a peace within ourselves.

The National Association of Child Development (NACD) out of Salt Lake City, Utah provides interesting alternative therapies that grabbed our attention. The director and founder, Bill Daman, believes that each child is unique in their learning style and abilities and that a child's education should be overseen by the parent. Their goal is to develop an individual program based on each child's needs. With only three therapies a week— in total—that were covered by medical insurance, Spencer was not able to progress like we'd want him to. So we made our first of many trips to Utah to be in the program.

Dr. Daman's evaluation rated gross motor skills, expressive language, fine motor skills, visual function, auditory function, and tactile function. Based on the seven levels of development in each category, Spencer was functioning at a level between one and three in most categories, except visual and auditory where he functioned at a level five and six. The exercises he would get would target all areas of the brain that had been affected by the encephalitis. Dr. Daman sent us home with a list of exercises to do three times a day, which would require nine volunteers per day. Unfortunately, insurance did not pay for this, so Russ and I asked our church members for volunteers. Miraculously, we started with 40 volunteers the first week of therapy, training three new people every three hours.

We made a video of family members completing the exercises with Spencer for the teaching and training of the volunteers. We didn't really know what we were doing, since we had just been trained ourselves. (Full disclosure here.) But if it would help Spencer make new connections in his brain, it was worth it. We would try it for four months and reevaluate the success rate in Salt Lake next summer.

While in Salt Lake we also saw a holistic naturopathic doctor who came highly recommended. He took a health history and did some testing on Spencer and found imbalances in his body. He suggested supplemental herbal formulas that would detoxify his body and build his immune system.

Our house was busy with people from 8 a.m. to 7 p.m. Our country home was on private land and stood majestically and wafted tranquility into your mental framework and, although like a dream-come-true from afar, it was anything but private. Despite the constant flutter, there was a vibrant life force that gave hope to everyone, lifting the heaviness of sorrow. It was as if our family had our own tribe of prayer warriors and counselors. And if it weren't for them, I'm not sure any of us would have made it through.

Our Elle developed more social experiences with adults than with her own peers. She was my trusty "people greeter" when I couldn't get to the front door. She addressed each visitor by name and showed them her newest plastic horse. Evan, who was always more introverted, watched from afar.

He'd engage only when he was drawn into conversation. With the nature of this routine, both kids yielded themselves to the environment around them: caring for a brother who needed minute-by-minute assistance, parents who needed to be on the spot—everywhere—and at all times, friends, family, and volunteers who needed enough understanding to cope and then to be able to help instead of hinder. It was baptism by fire.

48

Spring Synopsis, One Year Post Encephalitis

Our family Christmas letter was not really appropriate to share during glad tidings, so a spring annual letter was born. It was a quick review of a year never to be forgotten.

Happy Spring Family and Friends!

This year has presented us with our biggest challenge to date! As many of you know, we completed the construction of our new house and moved in by May 21. While still unpacking—nearly two weeks later, our 6-year-old, Spencer, began having low-grade flu-like symptoms, then seizures, and then he was overtaken with confusion. He suffered from tremendous migraine headaches, hallucinations, high agitation, which was ultimately followed by major confusion, by everyone. He lost speech, motor skills, and bladder control, yet no one could locate the "rewind" button! After numerous hospital visits, a CAT scan, two MRIs, an EEG, multiple spinal taps with assorted blood draws, they admitted Spencer to Denver Children's Hospital on our ten-year anniversary. Boy do we know how to celebrate!

We were far too busy to clink champagne glasses, as our boy's symptoms shipwrecked his body over the course of the next month. Test after test and doctor after doctor revealed nothing in his body that could have caused what they guessed to be viral encephalitis. The doctors figured he probably picked up some virus, germs on his unwashed hands perhaps, got in his mouth and went on into his bloodstream. It traveled past the blood-brain barrier, via spinal fluid, and without protest as earlier strep infections reduced his immunities altogether. Once in the brain, it spread like a ripple effect and caused overall cellular brain damage. His brain scan displayed a smaller brain with larger ventricles. And now the only thing that can be done for him is to try to retrain what's left of the good brain.

With brain injury every step is a big step. As long as there's progress, the brain needs consistent stimulation so that more connections can be made. Russ and I have had to go back to the baby days and try to remember what comes first. Eating then talking, creeping then crawling, walking then running. We do about 3-4 hours of therapy a day with volunteers, five days a week. Thank God for volunteers!

We are re-teaching Spencer how to swallow, creep, follow one step commands, get his eyes to track and see clearly, figure out where his body is in space...It will be an ongoing process that we can only take day by day. We will be back in Utah in June for re-evaluation.

We are all trying to accept Spencer's illness with grace and embrace him as he is. Despite Evan's heartache

over the little brother and playmate he knew, he is doing well in his new school and enjoys his friends and
scouting. Elle, my little nurse, is Spencer's #1 cheerleader and Mom's right hand gal. She enjoys her boy
friends at school and gets to be even more dramatic at
her tap, ballet, and tumbling class.

With the unbelievable support of family and friends,
God has carried us through this year. We would like
to send out a heartfelt thanks to all our volunteers and
prayer warriors who have been working their own
miracles and talking to God steadfastly throughout
this whole ordeal. Bless you!

We sincerely regret that we are confiding so much
sad news this year as we know it will be a shock and
disappointment to many of you. We hope that our
annual letters to follow will bring more uplifting news
to share.

We love you all. God bless you, and thank you for
keeping us in your prayers.

The McCombs Family

49

Hyperbaric Oxygen Therapy

October 2002

After nine months, a full gestation of doing re-patterning exercises, our Spencer was still at an infantile level of functioning. Our daily routine ran quite smoothly. Now that Nicole was part of the family and basically doing the majority of daily care for Spencer, it freed up my time to take care of the other two children and more family responsibilities.

I had some time for research and the newest therapy that had just come to town was Oxygen Therapy. Russ and I met with the doctors and decided that we would try 60 treatments, five treatments a week, Monday through Friday, one hour each day. Russ took Spencer one day, I went with him two days a week, my parents one day, and Nicole one day. The overall afternoon excursions lasted about three hours. It was considered an alternative form of therapy, so of course insurance did not cover it.

Russ was so patient and supportive in every therapy that I suggested and I was grateful for that. I would do the research, present my case, and say, "Now how do you propose we do this?" We always seemed to figure it out. He wanted to see improvement just as much as I did. The family business was doing well enough to cover many extras that were not covered through insurance. This was a huge blessing!

The Cellular Medicine Institute of America was the only freestanding hyperbaric oxygen facility in Colorado at the time. There were four chambers that were in use constantly during the three months that we were there. We met many people from Broncos players, to stroke victims, to children like Spencer who had been brain damaged from birth or from a traumatic injury.

Hyperbaric therapy works by forcing oxygen under pressure into the areas where blood flow is restricted. The therapy is usually administered once a day in 60-to-90 minute sessions for a period of two-to-three months. The intermittent nature of the therapy is to avoid oxygen toxicity while promoting healing. The oxygen allows for the formation of new blood vessels, which supply the damaged tissues. Patients can make remarkable progress even years after a stroke. HBOT is a treatment that gives the brain a blast of fresh air, repairing the effects of hypoxic brain injury.

HBOT is safe and painless, aside from the slight discomfort some patients feel at pressurization, and has no toxic elements. The patient simply lies in a clear acrylic chamber measuring approximately 8 by 3 feet while they breathe 100% pure oxygen as the entire chamber is slowly pressurized. I called it the bank deposit tube. That's what it reminded me of. Certified personnel monitor the entire treatment and most patients use the time to watch a movie, sleep, or listen to music.

Russ and I spent a few sessions in the chamber with Spencer and it was a snug fit. After we knew he could handle it on his own, we would sit with the technician during each session, watching closely for seizures or a need for suctioning (as Spencer did not swallow consistently). After my sessions I felt energized and my brain felt like it was much sharper, thinking more clearly.

While in the chamber, Spencer would get Glutathione treatments through and IV, three times a week. Glutathione is fundamental to the immune response and since Spencer's little body had been through traumatic insult from the virus, we felt it necessary to detoxify his body and it was said to help with digestion also. Spencer benefited from the GSH greatly.

After Spencer's first treatment, his eardrums got red from the pressure. We had to bring him out of the chamber early. Once home, he went into a half hour laughing fit. Spencer suffered a lot with daily trials, so when he laughed, so did we. It's been explained to us by other brain injured people who have recovered, that the brain just goes into this emotional state and all you can do is laugh. It also happens with crying. It's the brain's way of making new connections.

Being in this facility every weekday for three months gave us opportunities to meet so many interesting people and hear their stories of hope. Spencer's tech was a young guy named Trey. He was gentle, kind, loving, and my first counselor. It was the most time I had sat since we brought Spencer home from the hospital over a year ago. When Trey was sitting with Spencer, I just poured my aching heart out and asked many questions that a young man had no clue how to answer. At this point in our process, Russ had become somewhat of a workaholic—which I believe was a combination of feeling the financial responsibility for Spencer's care and a means of escape. I was feeling isolated in my grief and misunderstood. The fear that my boy would be this way for the rest of his life was getting stronger with each day that I saw almost no improvement.

Watching Trey sing the ABCs to Spencer as he transitioned down to the appropriate pressure warmed my heart. There was an emotional bond established through grief that was uncomfortable for me, to say the least. For Trey, I think he saw me as an older, wiser motherly type that was young enough to understand his generation. Shortly after HBOT, I began grief counseling and understood more fully that in my pain and need to be understood, my feelings for Trey became more than they should have. Russ and I discussed it through counseling. And so I learned that when a man and a woman go through crisis, they process grief very differently. It's important to get counseling in the midst of it, to get to the other side.

50

Community

"It takes a whole village to raise a child."
Igho & Yoroba Nigeria Proverb

"Hey Spencer, do you want a little cheese with that whine?" Larry (a therapy volunteer) would often say this when Spencer was not liking an exercise during therapy. Many times Spencer's whining would turn to laughter.

"Hi Buddy," said Bonnie, another volunteer. "Can you show me those beautiful brown eyes? Look here Spence. Hi…can you say 'hi?' watch my lips, buddy. Ha ha ha ha Hi. Say Hi." She would then pause, waiting for Spencer to make movement with his mouth or push air out. "Great job Bud. It's a beautiful day in the neighborhood. Give me a smile." Bonnie would try to get Spencer to talk each time she was with him. She believed with all her heart that Spencer would one day burst into full conversation.

"Spencer, can you push on my hand with your foot? Show me how strong your legs are. Come on. You can do it. Straighten your leg out. I know you can do it. Pretend like you are kicking a football." My Dad would be ever so patient and wait for purposeful movement from Spencer. If there was no response, he would help Spencer straighten and bend his leg and do range of motion with his hips, ankles, arms, and wrists.

"Here we go Spence. You ready? Hey, whataya doing upside down? You silly boy." This was often said by Pat when we would flip Spencer upside down on the inversion table. It helped straighten out his scoliosis.

"Hey Spencer, you want to wear my hat while you do the creep? You look better in it than me." Bill would try to take Spencer's mind off of the pain of the creep. This was when Spencer had to bear weight on all fours like a dog. He would have to hold that position with assistance for three minutes. It was exhausting.

"Okay Spence, you are going to see your photo cards; I need you to wake up. Open those eyes handsome!" My sister stroked his face and hair. "Wake up Buddy," she would say, "Hello, it's therapy time!"

"K, Spence, I am going to put my finger under your bottom lip. Can you close your mouth to swallow? Good job! See how it is easier to swallow with your mouth closed?" Nicole was the best at this. Not sure why he responded to her better than anyone else with his mouth exercises. His severe gag reflex made it difficult to do anything with his mouth. Our attempts would often make him vomit, but we tried anyway. If it meant that he could eat again on his own...I imagined him eating birthday cake.

"Oh Spencer, I am so sorry. Bless your heart buddy. Do you have a headache?" Many times this was said by Judy after witnessing a grand mal seizure. Sometimes all the stimulation of therapy put him over the edge. Therapy was over after a seizure.

"Spencer, it's time for your massage. You ready for Grandma to rub your back?" We always told Spencer what we were going to do before we did it to give him warning. He startled easily. His reward after therapy with Grandma, was a massage. He LOVES Grandma Charlotte's massages. He also loves Bonnie's massages (the family massage therapist).

One evening I went down to say good-bye to Spencer as I was leaving for date night. The volunteers were doing mouth exercises and I bent down to pick something up off the floor. I began to rise up when Spencer let loose and vomited into my hair. (It was a common daily occurrence. The good thing was that Spencer's vomit didn't smell like others since he only had juice in his stomach and it came up before it had time to ferment.) It was one of those days. I did not have time to completely wash my hair. I rinsed it out, changed my clothes, walked into the restaurant and told my husband not to touch or get too close to my hair. His quirky little smile was proof that he knew exactly what had happened. We became numb to the word "crisis". Our definition was a bit different from others, but when the day was done, we didn't want to talk about it. Living it was enough.

I was reminded of the phrase, "It takes a whole village to raise a child." That most certainly was true for our kids. With the attention that Spencer required, it was forever a challenge to balance the schedules of the rest of the family. If we had not had the support of nursing care, community and family, I am not sure where we would be today. There was a time where I was so overwhelmed by the constant stream of helpers, I threw my hands up in thanksgiving and asked, "Lord, how am I ever going to repay all these people?" I came to the conclusion, though I may not pay those specific people back, I would pay it forward when I could. God has honored that request.

I seriously could write a book on all the angels who have walked into our life with Spencer. This chapter will not cover them all, but you know who you are. We prayed that God bring us people who would understand and love Spencer the way we do, and He repeatedly answered this prayer. Spencer's care was complicated, so an efficient and loving caregiver was a small miracle. Volunteers for physical therapy, specialists, doctors, nurses, CNAs, teachers, aides, bus drivers, support groups, clergy, pastors, counselors, music therapists, friends, family...the list goes on. We shared a lot of time with these people over the years, but the people we got to know the best (besides Spencer's caregivers) were the volunteers who came to do Spencer's therapy Monday through Thursday. We began therapy in 2001, and still had eight of the original 45 in 2013. Larry Hoffman, Pat and Bill Logue, Carmen Slack, Judy Freuh, and my parents, Charlotte and Richard Swisher. These seven came faithfully every week for their scheduled hour and Spencer grew fond of each personality, as did the rest of the family. They also fell in love with Spencer and would often times join us for birthday parties or other events. In addition, we had a massage therapist and chiropractor come to our house biweekly. *Lord, thank-you for Alan Blaher and Bonnie Kilman.* The week we said our good-byes to our extended family, was difficult, to say the least.

Judy Freuh was especially imprinted on our hearts. When we met, she had recently lost a son in a car accident. After her second therapy session with Spencer, she poured out her heartache and I could barely hold back the tears. I thought to myself, *She is in such deep grief, there is no way I can expect her to come back and help us with Spencer.* I prayed about it and decided to let her make that decision. She was one of our most faithful angels and despite her heartache, I believe therapy with Spencer was also therapeutic for her. There was a moment in our discussions where I realized that had her son lived, he would have been more affected than Spencer—probably on a respirator. Seeing Spencer's care each week, I think Judy knew that though she missed her son greatly, he was in a better place. We shared the heartache of asking God, "why?" over and over again. Through the years, I think we resolved to let that question go, and found hope in the answer on the other side of heaven.

Nicole was also a therapy worker who turned into our Nanny/nurse for nine years. After the first year with Spencer, she approached me asking if I would consider hiring her part-time to help. Exhausted and living on adrenaline, I thought, *What a brilliant idea!* I presented her proposal to Russ and his dad agreed to pay Nicole out of the family business. Overnight, I had my own personal nurse, babysitter for Elle and Evan, supervisor for therapies, assistant for appointments, and the list goes on. Part-time became full-time and Nicole helped with everything.

One especially daunting task was making Spencer's food. Being tube fed, we decided to juice all of his feedings with fresh fruit and vegetables, making them into three recipes by adding fat and protein. We'd shop, juice, mix, and freeze individual bags of food—five 12 ounce bags for every day. This was a two-day job that we did every two weeks. For many years my folks juiced, and made Seal a Meal bags. I shopped for ingredients and Nicole would put the recipes together. This food was better than the milk based canned formula that was loaded with sugar.

Spencer was only in the hospital for three extended stays in 15 years! This is unheard of with a wheelchair-bound kid like Spencer. Each time we were there the doctors and nurses would ask what we were doing to keep him so healthy. I would share our recipes and supplements with them and reiterate that I believed his nutrition and therapies were the reasons for his sustained immune system and good health. After all, it was a Children's Hospital nutritionist who helped create the original recipe that we would tweak each year based on his blood work.

We all benefited from regular massage, chiropractic care, and grief counseling which was necessary to keep us healthy. My favorite new interest was a Hip Hop/Jazz dance class where I met four of my best girlfriends. Russ and I made it a point to go on a date night every Thursday and an out of town weekend every three months. We also planned a one-week vacation with Evan and Elle every year, leaving Spencer with Nicole. This provided quality time with the other two children without the underlying stress of Spencer's care. These trips sustained our marriage and our family bond.

51

Give Kids the World

January 26, 2002

It was 3:00 a.m. and the kids were dressed, bags ready to go. We would pull Spencer out of bed once the limo arrived. Evan and Elle were lying on the church bench in the foyer.

Headlights rounded the corner and illuminated our long driveway. Evan and Elle rushed toward the window with excitement.

"Good morning, you must be William," Russ said as he opened the front door.

"And you must be the McCombs Family. Are you ready to start your adventure with Give Kids the World?" he asked as he stepped inside to grab our luggage.

"Yes!" Evan and Elle exclaimed, jumping up and down with excitement.

Once they were all settled in the limo, we had to grab our Make a Wish boy, Spencer. He moaned in disapproval as we laid him on a makeshift bed in the limo.

The anonymous organization from our home town, furnished this all-expense-paid tribute to Spencer by giving us a sunshine beach trip to Florida!

When we were asked what Spencer's vacation wishes were, he smiled and lit up at the mention on Disney World, giving a grand slam "thumbs up" that we were counting on.

Pulling out of the drive, we raised our glasses of sparkling cider and toasted to our first family vacation in three years. Evan and Elle had been through a lot in the last year and a half and we needed to show them that they were just as important as Spencer. We were geared up to have two weeks of FUN in the SUN!

"Dear Guests,

I am Dr. Marty Martin, Chaplain for Give Kids the World Village. My hope and prayer is that this will be a special week for each of you.

We, the staff and our great group of volunteers, will do our best to help you enjoy the experience of a life-time. Give Kids the World Village is a community of love whose purpose is to make wishes and dreams come true.

I especially invite you to visit our Chapel sometime during your stay with us. It is a beautiful place for quiet meditation and prayer. I also offer my services as Chaplain. My office is in the Caring Center. Thank-you for allowing us to be a part of your life. God bless you and may your wishes come true."

Upon arriving at the GKTW Village, we got our welcome packet, tickets to Disney and Sea World, and we toured the grounds. Since Spencer's brain injury, this was by far the most special needs friendly environment we had been in. It was a welcome relief!

GKTW was a lovely place of respite for families struggling with terminal and long-term illness. It was a fun, safe, and a magical place to escape the realities of daily life. The kids especially loved the ice cream shack where they could indulge in an ice cream cone at any hour of the day or the movie theatre that you could slip into whenever you wanted a memory of a Disney prince or princess. There was also a train that chugged around the village that kids could ride at their leisure. The park and play room were happy places. We would go in and dress up as our favorite Disney character and read stories.

Mayor Clayton was a big overstuffed bunny that randomly visited each house in the village and tucked the little ones into bed. He arrived our first night there, and the kids enjoyed his story telling and games. Smiles and giggles filled the room. It was good to see the children so happy. Despite the fantasy fairy tale feeling, there was an undercurrent of grief for all visitors who walked through the gates of GKTW. A juxtaposition of sorts—terminally ill children set in a fantasy world.

Memories of our last vacation of three normal kids running on the beach resurfaced. The grief kept seeping into my consciousness. I had to compartmentalize and put on a happy face for the other two children. On my breaks,

I would sneak into the chapel and work on another layer of grief, mostly by asking God questions and journaling.

Our first evening in the cafeteria, we met the family sitting next to us. They had two children with a genetic disease, both in wheelchairs. Many of the other families we met had terminally ill children. We were reminded that things could ALWAYS be worse. This was the first time our crisis was comingled with many others and it was quite sobering. Yet, it was good for the kids to see the way others were dealing with their children. Every family's situation was unique; a story all their own. The GKTW neighborhood gave Evan and Elle an opportunity to know Spencer as his new self away from the stresses of home. Being introduced to similar situations helped them to feel less isolated in this new experience with a special needs brother. The blessings were overflowing, and that is what we decided to focus on.

My parents arrived to help us celebrate the next two weeks, making family memories with this new but different family dynamic. Nicole was also with us and got broken in quickly. With five adults

and three kids, we had all the help we needed for everyone to get a break from Spencer's constant care, get one on one time with each child, and have a good time. It was just what the doctor ordered. Prescription refill, PLEASE!

Disney World greeted us with a sign that read, "100 Years of Disney". We were stoked and even Spencer began to smile and rock back and forth, not being able to contain the thrill. After all the preparations to get there, it was a moment when we knew we did the right thing. We quickly snapped a bunch of pictures, knowing that one day soon our family would be seen in the future smiling right back at us in family photo albums. Twinkling eyes in happy times!

We skipped to the head of the line with our special Give Kids the World passes and boarded the Peter Pan ride. The operator told us that if Spencer wanted to go on the ride a second time to give him a thumbs up and he would not have to get off. Russ got Spencer out of the stroller and carried him up and onto the ride. I rode shotgun with our other two kids. Spencer smiled the whole time with bright eyes and even giggled a little. Russ gave the operator a thumbs up and they went around two more times. He especially loved the "It's A Small World" ride. This special occasion will be safely stored in our memories forever. Milestones!

After our week at the village we transferred to a beautiful nearby condo. Our departure was bittersweet, as the kids waved good-bye to the Village, Mayor Clayton, the train, and sighed over the endless churn of mouth-watering ice cream. They would talk about it for years to come. This vacation made each plucked heartstring turn to glorious music, deserving a story in the journal.

Sadly, we said our good-byes and extended our condolences to the family who was staying in the house next to us. They had experienced the death of their loved one while at Give Kids the World. We drove away with heavy hearts, asking God more questions.

Trips to Cocoa Beach and the Space Center, lying about the pool, playing putt putt golf, family karaoke night, and visiting other theme parks completed the trip. Russ and I savored as much R & R as we could get while Nicole and my parents toed the line on our behalf. Family karaoke night was complete with Russ singing, "Staying Alive" doing splits at the end. Evan sang, "Who Let the Dogs Out" with a never ending Chorus. Elle sang, "Get Down Tonight" which was totally inappropriate for a four-year-old but we laughed anyway. Russ and I closed the evening with "I Got You Babe" complete with Cher lip action and Sonny's Rico Suave voice.

The man who created Give Kids the World and the people who birthed Make a Wish Foundation have changed countless lives. We will be forever grateful for this experience and the people who support kids with long-term illness or terminally ill children.

52

Agony in the Garden

Summer 2002

The wise man in the storm prays to God not for safety from danger, but for deliverance from fear. It is the storm within which endangers him, not the storm without.

Ralph Waldo Emerson

The grief was coming in waves, but it was at bay; low tide. A crashing wave hitting a wall of rock at high tide was the fear that wore on me day after day. Fear that my other two children or husband might end up with a brain injury. And if that happened, I would never make it through. I had lost one child to the effects of brain damage. That was enough.

Each member of our family could be found embracing their passions. By now, we had all decided that life can change in an instant, never to be the same. "Why wait? Life is short, don't put off until tomorrow what you can do today. Embrace the passions of your heart." These were our family mottos.

So with that came flight lessons for Russ because becoming a private pilot was a lifelong dream. Russ flew for Angel Flight West as a way of giving back to those in need. It also gave him an opportunity to use his medical background. Elle began English riding lessons and I tagged along for that too. Evan, now ten, had a new motocross bike and so did Dad. Their summer project was to rebuild a go-cart junker to ride around our property. My first dance class at 37 years old was a challenge. It took all of my brain power—a fun escape from the day to day.

On the advice of a wise counselor, we sought out activities with our kids to build a tight relationship outside of Spencer's care. For the times that I fell away from God out of anger, each time Russ was in the air, Elle or Spencer on the back of a horse, or Evan on a motor bike, I prayed my way back.

Spencer was riding weekly, for HIPPO therapy. It helped strengthen his posturing and loosen up his high tone and spasticity. There was a day Jean, the trainer, asked the horse to go into a trot and excitedly the horse kicked up her heals. Even though there were two side walkers, Spencer still got bucked off. Adrenaline pulsating, I caught him by grabbing onto his side belt. When the weight of his upper body flipped him upside down, I pulled him up by one ankle before his head had a chance to touch the ground. Spencer's session was over. No harm done, but that's when you call it a DAY!

Elle was graceful riding her horse, going over jumps, and training for shows. Up in the air, she could let it all go… but I gasped to see my daughter sailing through the wind. Diverting my nerves to another view, what did I see but Evan airborne on his motor bike. Daredevils! I had to pray and turn around. I would have to work through this debilitating fear during counseling. I learned that if one does not work through their fears, they will manifest behaviors that may ultimately grow that fear into fruition.

One particular Saturday it was warm outside, and the go-kart and motor bike were moving in full force. From the back deck, I could see Evan and his friend coming straight toward one another. I envisioned a collision before me, sure as day. I stood there in terror as they passed each other. Whew!

I totally lost my cool. Russ lost his too and there we were, making a scene in front of the kids. *Exhale Angie, everyone is okay.* "Time to shut the vehicles down and come inside for dinner."

During dinner, adrenaline was pouring through my body. I felt as though I was having a heart attack. The symptoms would not go away. I excused myself and told my family I belonged at church. In the car, my breathing was shallow and I broke out in a panicked sweat over veins on fire. I walked into the midst of a prayer service, so I retreated to the "cry room". I was sitting on the edge of the seat, uneasy and unable to breathe. Listening to my heart sounding out furry and seeing stars, I slid to the floor. As I lay there, reduced to a pile of steam, I wondered if I should call 911. A million thoughts wanted to jam my circuitry, and I asked myself why the outbursts in front of the kids? It troubled me so. I was losing the ability to cope with my day to day. Once I took a few deep breaths, I felt my body start to calm and I was able to pray. My heart and breathing were slowing down. This was an episode of severe anxiety. I learned through the years that anxiety comes when one has unresolved grief.

The prayer service had ended. I walked into the sanctuary to be alone with Jesus. I dropped to my knees and closed my eyes.

There were times I looked heavenward to demand God's attention. "See US, Protect US, Do not betray US." I'd call out. I wanted answers from everyone because maybe they had come up with something better than the mysterious answers to all my "Whys?" Did they owe me an explanation, answers as to why God allowed this to happen to my child, my family, my life? I was grasping for resolution to an irresolvable problem. I just want to move on…into joy perhaps?

The hurt in my heart was smothering. I wore my masks well for most of the time, but the straps were getting worn and they were beginning to slide off my face. From soul to skin the anger would escape in droplets of steam and venom would come off my tongue. I no longer recognized myself; I couldn't find myself. I had become an exhausted, scared mother of three who was depressed and anxiety-ridden every day. My joy was fleeting and the guilt of finding it outside the household wore on me too. People were keeping their distance from me. I resolved to start letting the anger go, or it would take me down a dark path.

"Lord, I don't know how to go on living like this. I feel so alone in my grief. No one understands how heart wrenching it is to lose a son to brain damage and deal with this new, incredibly difficult child. Russ goes to work every day, the kids to school, while I am at home with Spencer. It's so exhausting. Lord, Spencer is not getting better. He is an infant in a 50-pound body. He is only going to get bigger, but will not progress into a child or even an adult. Unless there is a miracle, that is. Give us a miracle, God. Please! How am I going to live with this for the rest of my life? I'm only two years in, and I can barely function. I need to raise these two other kids. I need sleep. I need you to take my fear away. This fear is absolutely debilitating."

Right before me was a shadow of Jesus kneeling, looking up toward the vast heavens. I felt deeply moved. I blinked, tears coming up out of my throat. I stared at this beautiful sign. This was it, I had lost my mind. There was no one there, even now, to help me in this desperate moment. Doesn't God want me to rely on Him even in my darkest hours? Yes!

I continued to stare at the "vision" that I was now convinced He had given me. It was another part of our story, I was sure of that. I didn't understand it, but I embraced the moment and continued to breathe. God would clue me in later.

Still kneeling in silence, the woman who was closing up the church asked, "Angela, do you need a few more minutes?"

"Do you mind?" I asked.

"No, not at all. Let me know when you are leaving."

"Okay, thank you."

I looked back and the shadow was gone. *Where have I seen this picture of Jesus before?*

"I will never leave you nor forsake you, Angela." I heard...but I wasn't sure if I was listening to my conscience speaking or the Holy Spirit? "I will never leave you Angela, I hold you now, I cry with you."

"Thank you Jesus." I was not ALONE!

Between the kids and their dangerous sports, snarling with my husband, fatigue for the never ending care of my fragile boy, I'd had an overload of drama for one evening. Looking at the clock, my responsibilities at home were calling me back. It was the children's bedtime.

The weekend couldn't come quick enough. My parents were downsizing and moving in a week. I got a chance to spend time in the house where I grew up. I lay in my childhood bedroom surrounded by the joyful yellow walls and cheerful floral border. Many memories rushed in. I spent many hours writing in this room and there was no better place to catch up on my weekly journal. I put pen to paper until my hand lost circulation. Journaling, since I was ten, was always my favorite thing to do to touch on what I was feeling. Rereading my journals gave me insight into what I had to understand and overcome. They also showed me how much I had grown over the years and assured me that God does in fact answer prayers.

My vision at church was my journal entry which led me to the Bible. After I read about Jesus' time in the garden, it was as if I had never heard this story before. My bleeding heart needed healing, and this scripture was my tourniquet for the night. Several months before, I had contemplated suicide. Deep sorrow engulfed me, exhaustion, anxiety, and no end of this difficult life was in sight. The thought was fleeting as I had to go home and host a five-year-old horsey party for Elle. My friend, Cathi was with me and talked me off the ledge. She was not only my horse riding buddy, accountability partner, but now my life saver, "literally". She pulled me out of the pit and onto the back of a dogsled. I wasn't in this place anymore, but I still had to live moment by moment, day by day.

Luke 22: 39-46 NIV

Jesus went out as usual to the Mount of Olives, and his disciples followed him. On reaching the place, he said to them, 'Pray that you will not fall into temptation.' He withdrew about a stone's throw beyond them and knelt down and prayed, 'Father, if you are willing, take this cup from me; yet not my will, but yours be done.' An angel from heaven appeared to him and strengthened him. And being in anguish, he prayed more earnestly, his sweat was like drops of blood falling to the ground.

When he rose from prayer and went back to the disciples, he found them asleep, exhausted from sorrow. 'Why are you sleeping?' He asked them. 'Get up and pray so that you will not fall into temptation.'

After reading the passage my revelations poured into my journal. Jesus was HUMAN just like me. There are many differences, but the main one being that I am a sinner. How did he not sin? I'd want to whack his disciples upside the head. If I were Jesus my thoughts would be, "Dudes, wake up. You are my very best friends. We've shared some difficult, amazing, and intimate times together over the last three years. In fact, we just shared our last Passover meal together. You can't even stay up with me at my darkest hour? Do you realize I am dying tomorrow for the salvation of the world? I am really scared right now; can you just sit with me and pray? Our time is coming to an end."

I can imagine that the disciples had their bellies full of food and wine, and it was their bedtime. But really? I think often times people don't realize the value of a person until they're gone. Was this true, even for Jesus?

"Take this cup from me Father." Yep, I have prayed that many times. Can so relate to that passage. Fear of the unknown can be so unnerving.

"Yet not my will, but yours." Isn't that what it always comes down to? Our will versus God's? Honest to God…I am so un-reconciled to my life. Do I believe that I am able to rise to what is asked of me? I wasn't sure why I was chosen as Spencer's mother, but I had to trust that God knew. And I would walk this life out with Spencer, Evan, Elle, and Russ if that is what He was asking me to do. As tiring as it was to tell Spencer's story over and over again, I made a vow to

God that night that I would tell it to whoever asked. That was my mission in life and one day I would write the book He told me to write. God would have to give me all things necessary...for now, faith and strength.

The SON OF GOD himself felt so alone at His darkest hour. Why should I be exempt from suffering if Jesus suffered? Will I remain in my state of self-pity and depression, or can I use what I have learned to change the world?

The gist of my vision of Jesus in the garden, came down to the fact that he felt scared, misunderstood, and abandoned too. In my grief and contemplation of it, I have decided that Americans are not properly taught how to grieve. I have studied other cultures to come to a better understanding of grief and the importance of going through the steps, but not staying there. I know now that my expectations of others are sometimes unfair. When the ones I love fall off of the pedestal I have placed them on, I am back on my knees, looking upward.

"Be strong and courageous. The Lord himself goes before you and will be with you; He will never leave you or forsake you. Do not be afraid; do not be discouraged."

1Deuteronomy 31:7-8

53

Dr. Carragg

Fall 2002

One morning after my quiet time, I walked into the kitchen and had a revelation about a lead that I'd gotten on a doctor, but hadn't looked into. Our dwindling choices reduced the options left available to fewer and fewer over the course of two and a half years. We were running on empty in terms of energy, perseverance and hope. Where was that business card of that chiropractic neurologist, that someone had handed to me a long time ago? I surveyed my pile of rolodex cards that were shoved in a drawer. There it was scribbled on the corner of an old church bulletin, Dr. Carragg from the Carragg Institute in Florida. No time like the present, so I picked up the phone.

"Carragg Institute, this is Serena, Can I help you?"

"I have a son who was severely brain injured two and a half years ago from the effects of viral encephalitis and was wondering about Dr. Carragg's program and if it would help him in any way." I inquired.

Serena asked me a number of questions to gain more information. "Would you like to talk with Dr. Carragg? This doesn't happen very often, but I believe he is actually sitting in his office right now."

"Uh, sure. I guess." I had no idea who this guy was or what he did, but it was worth a try as I had nothing to lose. He explained that he is a chiropractic neurologist. Sounded interesting to me, holistic medicine meets western medicine.

I spent the next 20 minutes telling the condensed version of our life with Spencer, going back to the summer of 2000. Dr. Carragg clarified by asking follow-up questions and said that he worked with individuals with the most difficult to diagnose and with the most severe neurological syndromes. Dr. Carragg was *especially* interested in the cases that were difficult to diagnose. He took referrals of people from all over the world and the clinicians would participate in their examination, diagnosis, and treatment.

Unfortunately, he confessed, there are only places for 50 patients and a placement assignment was made only after a panel evaluates the severity and need to be seen in "Grand Rounds". By the end of the conversation he asked us to come to Grand Rounds in Oslo, Norway in January. This conference would host specialists from all over the world. He was convinced that the new discoveries he'd made on retraining the brain could help our Spencer.

I spent the next two hours researching Dr. Carragg and was intimidated by his accolades and accomplishments. One of which was the PBS special on these treatments entitled WAKING UP THE BRAIN: AMAZING ADJUSTMENTS which had been viewed around the world with great acclaim. This film featured Dr. Carragg's work, highlighting the successful treatment of the most difficult neurological cases that had failed under traditional medicine. My hope meter began to travel from a negative ten to mach

100 in minutes! I was now considering a better future for my son, and *his* case might be heard in Oslo.

It was time to put my sales hat on and convince my husband and tell my parents to start praying. Was it worth the effort and expense of another few thousand dollars since all the expenses would not be paid? We prayed and asked God for a quick answer, but in my experience, God has no reference for time, being that He is eternal. The signs we were getting pointed us toward Norway. Or was it our hope or "false hope" as some call it, that was speaking into our consciousness? Nevertheless, we gave Dr. Carragg our "yes" and kept praying. We'd be going to Oslo in January, with Spencer!

First, I had to go on a much needed girl's trip to Cozumel with my lifelong friend, Tami. The week vacation, free of the responsibilities of three children, was a godsend. I became Angie again and rediscovered my adventurous spirit I'd been missing. Snorkeling and swimming with the dolphins, lazing on the beach, scooters around the island, road trip down the coast of Riviera Maya, discoveries in Tulum, great food and conversation, re-established my purpose and well-being while I was there. Admittedly, it was hard to come back to the craziness of the McCombs household.

I came up with a slogan a week later. "When Mom plays, Mom pays." I arrived home to a sick Evan who was ill all week. Poor buddy. He was also having teacher issues and I think maybe I let him stay home a couple extra days to get a break from the drama. Russ was extra busy at work due to the ground breaking for the expansion on the building. On Tuesday, I left the sink on in the laundry room (no drain) and went to answer a phone call. Two hours later, it was raining in our basement storeroom. On Wednesday, I went to start the van and the heater was not working. Sixteen hundred dollars later, we were advised that the mice had packed two pounds of dog food into the heating system. The joys of living in the country! The next day, I picked up our van after its maintenance and was en-route to get groceries when Russ called. He wanted to meet on the other side of town, to shore up the plans for Norway. Quickly, I turned around and within a mile, a young man pulled out in front of me and I hit him going 30 mph. Everyone was okay, but by now my fuse had burned to the end and it was starting to flame.

The officer came up to the driver's side window. "Ma'am, you need to get out of your car to fill out this paperwork because the damage is millimeters from your airbag sensor and it may blow at any second."

"Officer, can you believe this? I just paid $1,600 to get dog food out of my heating system, turned around to head back across town and now this? How much do you think this will cost me? I'm so ticked off right now. I just want to go back to Mexico!" I huffed.

Trying not to laugh the officer said, "Ma'am, you need to get out of your car. Please, you can sit in the back and do this paperwork. It's for your safety. You sure you are okay? No pain anywhere?"

"No, I'm fine."

Then there was soon-to-arrive Thanksgiving and Christmas to get through. The weeks following were filled with holiday festivities, emails back and forth preparing for the conference, and the daily activities that kept us constantly busy.

Our passports were ready and it was time to head to Norway. Evan and Elle stayed with my brother and his family. I often wondered how they felt being left behind when we had to go on another trip, seeking treatment for Spencer or even when we went away as a couple. We had to refuel so we could continue what our life required. I hoped it would not affect the other two in a negative way. I prayed that they would feel carefree and have a good time with my brother's family.

54

Oslo, Norway

January 2003

On the flight to Paris, Russ, Nicole, and I took turns sitting next to Spencer. He needed constant propping up, as his posture was not sustainable on his own. When it was time for him to sleep, we would lay him across our laps as comfortably as possible. While others around us slept, we connected his feeding tube, change his pants, and clothes, etc. It was difficult to use the suction machine in the airplane as there was not an electrical outlet. So we would have to prompt Spencer to cough, removing his secretions manually. Coach seating provided us with much more opportunity to share our story and educate those brave ones curious enough to ask about the care of a significant needs child. It was a fulltime job, and I was grateful that we had three people to do it!

Welcome to Paris! Architecture, romance, art. Arrival in the Paris airport was chaos! Apparently, this was normal. Sixteen months post 911, security was extremely tight. As I sat inside a curtained station with Spencer on my lap, they took his stroller apart piece by piece. Reassembling proved to be a bit more difficult. Nicole and Russ patiently waited, then got up to explore the airport. My mind rewound to that fateful September day. I sat and prayed for healing, peace, unity…love.

With the delay in security, we barely made our bus and literally ran to catch it. Russ and Nicole charged the back door and grabbed the front wheels of Spencer's stroller as I lifted it from behind. We nearly got closed in the door, before it started moving. We were off and running! Moments away from shut eye, after a night flight was a relief. Traveling through the busiest roundabout in Europe was an experience that was optioned as an actual insurance coverage choice! Crazy! *Note to Tourists: if you drive in Paris, take the last right hand turn before the roundabout!*

We finally arrived at our hotel and quickly realized that Paris is not a handicapped friendly city. It is beautiful, but the centuries-old buildings and walkways are difficult to navigate. Every space is compact and not easily accessible. We'd definitely over packed and learned our lesson there. It was early morning when we arrived and a power nap of about five hours gave us enough energy to make a trip to the Eiffel Tower and enjoy a nice Parisian dinner on the Champs-Elysees. It was a frigid day and we needed to make sure Spencer would stay strong, so he and Nicole remained in the suite away from chilly drafts and wintery air. He'd probably sleep for the next three days, seriously! Not wanting Nicole to miss out, Russ did the Eiffel Tower and dinner again with her. Afterward, we all napped and were up to visit the Notre Dame Cathedral before catching our flight to Norway. Not too bad for a 36-hour layover. I really wanted to see the Louvre, so I'd have to return.

The country of Norway is beautiful, clean, and really seems like one of the last frontiers on earth. The people were polite with utmost etiquette and manners, and were helpful in every way. I have no complaints about our short visit, and in fact, I would love to return. We arrived in the early evening and got settled into our hotel which was minutes from the Rainbow Vika Konference Centre in Oslo. The conference would require all our energy the next day, so just as Spencer was nodding off, we also took the opportunity to sleep. When Spencer sleeps, it's smart to follow his lead as he has no reference for night or day.

We showed up a half hour before Spencer's scheduled time. Dr. Carragg would be conducting many eye exercises; however, Spencer was weary from the travel and was presently deep in REM sleep. No one could wake him up and we tried everything. Seeing our frustration, a kind young vibrant chiropractor from Texas came over to assist us. With his Texas twang he sweet-talked Spencer and sang while he rubbed his legs. That got Spencer's complete attention!

The evaluation lasted for about 30 minutes. Dr. Carragg had Russ, Spencer, and I come up on stage in a huge lecture hall that held about 300 people. He started with some questions about Spencer's condition and his progress since the initial insult. Then there were questions about his normal years and what kind of kid he was. Dr. Carragg told the audience the exercises he was going to do with Spencer and then tried to do them. Much of his evaluation had to do with watching the movement of Spencer's eyes. Based on tracking and the direction they moved, he could tell us more specifically about the functionality of Spencer's brain. After I held Spencer's head and repeatedly asking him to open his eyes, Dr. Carragg didn't get much accomplished. We explained his exhaustion from the travel. Dr. Carragg understood, and we would need to return tomorrow. The whole exercise was a bit frustrating because we had no control over getting Spencer to cooperate. Ironically, he definitely had a mind of his own.

The next day Spencer cooperated a bit more. At least he was awake! Russ and I were more at ease as well, since we now knew what to expect. Because our level of uncertainty directly affected Spencer—it was as if he could just *feel* us—he settled because we got settled. Once the doctor finished, he went on to the next patient, and we anxiously awaited the outcome of the evaluation.

Within the hour the doctor finished up and came to talk with us. He was gentle, kind, real, and sincerely wanting to help our boy come to a greater functionality. What he said surprised me. Based on where Spencer's brain was at, we were doing TOO MUCH! We were over stimulating him and we needed to back off to one therapy a day and let him be a little boy. Focus on our other two children before we lost them to the psychological effects that can take over from growing up with a significant needs sibling. If there was no other reason that we went to Oslo, it was worth it for those TWO reasons alone. Some of the best advice we had gotten, by far.

We now had permission to quit chasing cures, spending astronomical amounts of money, and me living my life at appointments, therapies, and healing services. It was time to come to a status quo in the life of Spencer Lee and be happy there; maintain what we had with his health and abilities, and nurture our marriage, Evan, and Elle. I breathed a sigh of relief! It was time to give the control back over to God, who I'd been angry with for two and a half years.

Our Norway salutations to family and friends:

As many of you know, when there is an ongoing hardship in your life, it takes on a life of its own and sometimes talking about it becomes more impossible at every turn. But we are pleased that everyone wants to know of any news, because that shows you care. We thought this would be the quickest, simplest way to share.

Our little soldier, Spencer, has seen between 30-40 doctors in hopes of getting help for his healing. We came to Oslo, Norway for an evaluation by Dr. Carragg on January 10, 2003. He is a noted chiropractic neurologist who has researched more about the brain than any other doctor we've worked with. He has hope that Spencer will eat, walk, and talk again. He says that Spencer's outcome is limitless. I like his optimism! He has seen kids that are far worse than Spencer who progressed back to normal. Naturally, we welcome any improvement for his quality of life.

Dr. Carragg is the only doctor who has seemed to look at the whole picture of Spencer's condition and has taken into consideration how his early ailments may have led to the low immune system which in turn led to the viral encephalitis. He believes that Spencer's immune system has always been low and that his cerebellum could have been damaged as a baby by two ruptured eardrums in the same night. Dr. Carragg will take some of the exercises we do and fine tune them to work specific areas of the brain that he knows are blocked. He says we may be doing too much therapy and that Spencer needs to focus on all the kid boy things. We will now include him more often with the other children's activities. We breathed a sigh of relief!

After the consultation we had with Dr. Carragg, he met with a colleague who also attended the conference and was invited to review Spencer's case. Dr. Carragg and Dr. Englebrech then created a program that she will be able to introduce to Spencer on her quarterly trips from Texas to Aspen. After we meet with her, we will have new information to bring to you. Until then, thank you for all your prayers.

Russ, Angie, Evan, Spencer, and Elle

Our follow up letter, February 2003

Family, friends, and volunteers,

Our follow-up from Norway was on Jan. 17th and 18th up in Aspen, Colorado, only four days after returning from Oslo. We took the whole family and had a fun time at the Hot Springs in Glenwood. We are excited to be learning new, specific exercises that trigger the part of the brain that will help facilitate chewing and swallowing and develop more tongue and muscle movement in the mouth. If the exercises are successful, we might get Spencer eating by mouth sooner. If he can get these skills down, then many other skills will follow. We will see Dr. Englebrech again in approximately two months to see if there has been progress. Fingers crossed, prayers prayed.

Through the testing in Norway and Aspen, we have learned that Spencer's left side of the cerebellum (like a smaller brain at the base of the skull) is working better than the right. Exercises attempt to stimulate the right side of the cerebellum to catch up to the left side. The mesencephalon (middle part of the brain that helps with chewing and swallowing) will be stimulated too. So this could be a win-win situation!

When Spencer's pulse goes up and oxygen goes down, it shows that his brain is being overstimulated. We are to stop and let him rest when this occurs because when his brain is revved up too high, overworked brain cells start shutting down. This explains to me a reason for Spencer's inconsistencies from saying "Hi" last June to not slobbering for two weeks and swallowing really well, to slobbering again. The doctor also cautioned us not to overstimulate auditorily and visually because he is hypersensitive in those areas.

Dr. Englebrech said Spencer's left side is more rigid than his right side. This means his involuntary muscles (the muscles used for posturing) are not working as well on that side. High tone can be confused with strength. Strength has to do with moving muscles and tendons on a voluntary level vs. involuntary. If we see progress in two months, we move forward. If not, the two doctors' theory did not work on Spencer and we'll have to make do with what we have learned so far. We'll give another update in a few months.

Thanks for caring, reading, and praying-
Russ, Angie, Evan, Spencer, and Elle

By the end of summer, we had decided that their theory did not work on Spencer, as significant improvements were not apparent. We were disappointed once again. We tapered off on exercises and found a more satisfying balance by participating in family activities *together*. Milestones!

PART V

CALM WAVES AND UNDERCURRENTS

*"Only one difference between the race of human life
and the waves of the ocean, the ocean is never tired."*
Tanmaya Guru

55

Nicole

Spencer-Happy 14th Birthday. I wrote this poem in honor of you and submitted it in a poetry contest. To me and those who love and know you...You are a Beautiful Boy whose strength, grace and love inspire us all. I only hope and pray to live a life as worthy to the glory of Christ's name as you have thus far! I love you Beautiful Boy, Spencer!

BEAUTIFUL BOY
by Nicole

Most hearts and minds miss your immeasurable worth,
To me you embody, love, grace, and hope's birth.
Your life involves great burdens, a heavy cross to bear,
The vomit, the seizures, the confines of your wheelchair.
You are bathed, dressed, cajoled to swallow and chew,
Your eyes speak your "thanks" and "I love you."
Seemingly nothing to offer or give,
Blind hearts might deem you unworthy to live.
Oh, Beautiful Boy, strength and value unknown,
Through your humble dependence my faith has grown.
The Suffering Servant, he too was lowly,
Humbled on the cross of His majesty.
Your calling has pointed me straight to Him,

Author of life, love and Healer of limbs!

For nine years, Nicole was our right hand gal, nanny, mommy #2, nurse, launderer, errand girl, physical therapist, my assistant, and counselor. The woman is a saint. She listened to me blathering on—sometimes all day—about every topic… including the past, the history with me and my girlfriends, marriage, the house, and of course Spencer, Evan and Elle. She entertained neighbor kids and was a host to visiting relatives and friends. "Chief Many Hats" broke up fights when the kids were brats, and remarkably enough, she even trained for a marathon running Spencer, in his stroller along every dirt road in our neighborhood. She managed missions workers during my parent's 50th anniversary party, went with us to Paris, Norway, Disney World, Aspen, Utah. She fed horses, dogs and cats and did enough laundry and ironing for two lifetimes. She mustered up for babysitting so that the two of us could have date nights and romantic getaways. And if this weren't enough, she was Spencer's primary caregiver 40 hours a week on a nine-year stretch! Did I mention she is a saint?!

I call Nicole our saving grace; our angel. There is no doubt that God brought her to our family and kept her there for so long. There was nothing easy about her job. I believe it was the love and connection she had with Spencer and her relationship with God that kept her with us. She is one of the most Christ-like people I know.

The job of caregiver that we hired Nicole for was definitely her sweet spot. No one to this day has the deep connection with Spencer that Nicole does. Russ and I have a special connection as his parents, but her relationship with Spencer is different. Just like the mystery of the silent communication between my boy's mind and the world around him, their communication goes far beyond our understanding.

My favorite times to watch their interaction was when Nicole would read, sing or pray with Spencer. He listened intently or was lulled to sleep by the soothing sound of her voice. Spencer's whole demeanor relaxed and became peaceful at the first recognition of Nicole's voice or presence. She was his calm in the storm, his safety net, his rock. One of their favorite things to do was sit on the porch while the other kids played outside. Nicole would explain to Spencer what was happening and often times get the others involved by having them come interact with him. She so badly wanted for Spencer to partake in some normalcy of childhood playtime. On nice days, Spencer would accompany them on the basketball court, and loved it! Nicole included Spencer in Evan's and Elle's lives as much as he would tolerate. Many times we would come home from date night to see Spencer sitting at the table "helping" Elle or Evan with homework. Stalling bedtime routines included horsey gallops, video games, and sibling rivalry, "fighting" which usually sent Spencer into uncontrollable laughter

Nicole is the person who knew Spencer the best after his brain injury. After all, she was with him the most consistently during the day. When all others wanted to run from the intensity and exhaustion of our life, she was there to embrace him just as he was. In 2009, our family was in Sonoma, California at my niece's wedding. I had a premonition at the end of the reception that something was about to happen. At 6 a.m. the next morning, we got a call that Spencer had labored breathing and was being taken to Children's Hospital. He was later admitted for pneumonia. Nicole had to manage that all on her own and I felt helpless and guilty, being so far away. Where the mysteries left her questioning how to help this suffering boy, she was on her knees asking God for help. Less than 24 hours later I walked into ICU. To my right was

Spencer on a breathing tube and Nicole on the makeshift bed praying with her pastor.

Nicole will always be one of my favorite people. I will forever be grateful for the ability to have Nicole as our right hand girl for all those years. She was the second Mommy in the house. Did I say she is an angel? There are no words to express the amount of gratitude we have for her service to our family. All I know is that her crown will be filled with jewels when she gets to heaven.

After Nicole had given her two weeks-notice in late 2010, the idea of saying good-bye broke our hearts. Her willingness to jump in to fill any and all gaps to be the glue that holds all the pieces together, will not be forgotten. We knew it was time for her to move forward, so we wished her the best life under God's care and knew she would have it! Saying good-bye to our household superstar meant that we'd rely on God's grace to bring us a new angel to care for Spencer.

Nicole went on to Nanny for several other families. She continues to serve others, selflessly, knowing that this is her mission in life. We love you Nicole and miss you so much!

56

Spencer

A letter to Spencer on his twelfth birthday:

Sweet Spencer,

You are not the same boy we danced with when you were six. In many ways you are more. You have taught our family so much. Though your body does not function the way you would like, your warrior spirit makes up for that. If we never get to dance again on earth, our time will come. In heaven there is no pain, no suffering, no seizures. You will be whole and rewarded for what you did on Earth as God's humble servant. There we can dance joyfully for all eternity.

Spencer Lee, God created you special. You have taught us patience, perseverance, compassion and to never give up. In every situation you strengthen our faith, hope, and love. Our family has learned to work toward our passions, make bucket lists, and embrace life to the fullest. You have reminded us to work on defeating the Goliaths in our lives,

instead of letting them beat us down. We have learned that
a person's mind, will, and emotions (soul) have the ability to
heal the human body.

Your relationship with our Creator fills our spirits with
light to move forward through our darkest days. Spencer,
through your spirit, we believe that the supernatural touches
our lives daily. We feel that God gives you special graces to
see what we cannot because you are trapped inside your body
and mind. Through it all we have learned that God is the
biggest comedian of all and shows us when to laugh at our
mistakes and embrace his humbling lessons.

We thank God for each day with you Sweet Spencer.
Each improvement you make is a miracle to us. You are our
Bug, our angel on earth, our saint Spencer. We love you from
the deepest parts of our hearts-

To the moon and back,

Your family.

Spencer's daily schedule did not change much. We tried
a few more therapies and supplemental formulas through the
years, but overall we did just what Dr. Carragg had suggested:
scale back to what Spencer could handle, and focus on gaining
a *new normal*. He was RIGHT! This is exactly what the
doctor ordered, and it worked. Who knew that this was the
REAL reason we went all the way to Norway?

Spencer was never a morning person when he was
young and this never changed. His perfect day is from noon
to midnight, just like Mom. We spent many nights reading,
watching TV, or just plain talking while everyone else slept.
There were many nights he sat in the kitchen amidst my

girlfriends. We all decided that when Spencer's miracle comes, he needs to write a book devoid of all our inappropriate stories that he LOVED! Spencer sat quietly, voiceless and we often forgot he was there, until he burst into laughter, usually over a naughty word, or dramatic story.

In the shower chair at 8 am, warm water was usually his wake up call. He hated showers, which meant, *so did we.* There was nothing easy about them. Brushing his teeth usually induced vomiting. Fighting his tight and rigid arms to expose his armpits for washing was painful. And prying tight fists open and straightening his contracted wrists to rid them of the *cheesy* smell, took time, patience, and a gentle touch. All the while, cold air rushed in through the partially opened door. It was irritating to his skin and an overstimulating experience! Spencer whined the whole time. If it's true that misery loves company, he got two for the price of one. I'd often let water wash over my face to hide my tears. The warm water without touching was his favorite and the whining would subside. Showers could be his best or his worst time of the day.

The highlight of Spencer's day was in therapy with the people he adored! He also loved being with peers at school, but most of the time the environment invited too much chaos. The teachers recognized this and took him to his own private space. From August to December he went fairly regularly, but through the winter when illness was moving from one child to another, we kept him home. With Spencer's delicate immune system, our life as a family came to a screeching halt whenever he got sick.

Spencer sometimes snored during dinner which would make us all chuckle. At other times he would interact with us. Often we would ask him questions about his day. An "UH" usually meant it was okay, the norm. A moan usually meant, "leave me alone, I am sleeping," and a giggle or laugh usually meant, "It was an especially good day. Or maybe I am laughing at something you guys said." These moments when Spencer had a voice were few and far between. We always longed for more.

We tried to have him up as much as possible during the day, so he would sleep at night, but in the end, Spence made his own schedule. He slept on average, 10-12 hours a day. If he was having seizures, was sick, had anesthesia, or had traveled, he could sleep for two days straight. Oddly enough, he would fly out of orbit every anniversary of when he first got sick (June) then again around Christmas. During these emotional times of the year, he would have more seizures. Then he would sleep off and on for a week.

How did he know? Even if he didn't have memory of the virus attacking his brain, did his body remember it? Or did he possess enough mind to relive the memory? Maybe he could feel the energy of all of us reliving it. Whenever any one of us would tell his story, and he was within earshot, he would get agitated and throw a temper tantrum. We had to be careful what we said in front of Spencer and remind others to hold back. Just because he doesn't talk, doesn't mean he doesn't grasp meanings of words being spoken.

In 2005 we all went to Maui for a family trip. We realized after this that it was too much for Spencer to travel. Several days after arriving we were still catching up from the jet lag given us by Spencer's sleeping pattern. My sister Carmen came with us as she is a nurse. It was nice to have three adults, so when one stayed behind with Spencer, Elle and Evan each had their own adult companion. The view off the deck was a postcard of volcanic rock beaches with trade winds carrying in the scents of Plumeria and Gardenia.

We brought along two weeks' worth of Spencer's frozen juice meals… all 65 bags of it! Somehow Aloha airlines lost the cooler somewhere between the thirty-minute flight from Maui to Kauai so Spencer had to live on V8 until it was found eight hours later. On a two-week vacation, with three kids, this was the only mishap. Not counting a minor exception the week before when Elle snapped her collarbone. But still…Not bad!

Spencer's most favorite excursion is when we visited Hanalei Bay in Princeville. We sang "Puff the Magic Dragon: on the way. He loved it! He was wheeled up on the beach and stared out into the ocean for hours. He watched the kids skim board and splash in the water to their hearts' content. We took him out waist deep so he could experience the ocean. I felt Spencer's excitement and fear as we neared the water.

"Relax Spencer, it's okay. Mom and Aunt Carmen have got ahold of you. We will not let you go. You are safe."

I wasn't sure if the powerlessness that he felt or the overwhelming stimulation of the waves caused his whining. We listened to his clues and retreated back to our chairs on the beach to dry off in the sunshine.

Nevertheless, it was a peaceful place to recognize another lost and beloved soul as the undercurrent of emotion from the recent passing of Grandma Jan was heavy on our minds. The beauty that surrounded us was a gentle reminder of the beautiful person we had lost and the perfect place to start the healing of our broken hearts.

In 2009, Spencer went to the hospital with pneumonia while we were at a wedding in California. He had labored breathing and a fever. I was there within 12 hours of the phone call and felt awful that Nicole had to handle this all on her own. We gave her the next two weeks off, as she was quite shaken. We had not adequately prepared her for a situation like this. Russ and I would alternate 24-hour shifts until he was released. We would not leave him alone.

The first week was touch and go. I listed Spencer on prayer chains, prayed constantly myself, but then retreated to a room down the hall to see if I could get a few hours of sleep. One night brought me to my knees with an insurmountable fright! I was convinced that we may very well lose Spencer. After all we'd been through, I don't know how I'd handle that! I lowered my head and prayed. Just when I released my fears to God, I could feel an overwhelming peace shower down over me. It was a peace that surpasses understanding. I felt the presence of others praying for our family. It got me through the next week.

Spencer was in ICU rigged up on a breathing tube for five long days. They were giving him bags of fluid, but not feeding him because of the risk of aspiration. His fever came down and he started breathing on his own, with the help of additional oxygen. After moving him from ICU, I was urging the staff to give him food. His body was getting weaker and he was starting to have seizures. After an episode with staff concerning his recovery, we had a meeting with the doctors. I told them, "Spencer's basic needs are not being met. He is not eating, nor sleeping, and is sedentary. How is his body supposed to heal? If you are fearful that he will aspirate, I will sign a waiver taking responsibility so that he can have food." They agreed and within two days after feeding Spencer, he was released. He needed oxygen for about a month, but then healed completely. Thank you Lord!

This was the only extended hospital stay Spencer had in 14 years post encephalitis. We were proud to say that we took exceptional care of him. Our caregivers were highly aware of our expectations and our constant communication and daily checklists let nothing slip through the cracks. Since it was a compromised immune system that led to the brain damage, I would protect it vehemently. If his body was healthy, hopefully his brain would heal.

Often people think having a brain injured family member is better than losing them altogether. We often discussed this idea when it was raised, but we knew beyond a doubt that Spencer was with us for a reason. Losing someone to brain damage is a loss of the person you once knew, as well as the loss of oneself. The metamorphosis from the one you knew and loved to a person changed, requires deliberate patience and painstaking attention…all the time knowing full well they cannot return to the same way they once were. The dynamics of the relationship changes drastically and is more often ended as the change is too hard to handle; it's just too heart wrenching.

Why Spencer remains in this world as he is, is a question I addressed in my prayers. "Why is he still here Lord? What is his purpose?"

And God astounded me. "Spencer is a teacher and intercessor for others." Amazing. So I began to wonder in which way he had taught those around him. I was only just starting to figure out how he was teaching me, so I decided to ask how Spencer changed the lives of others. That is a subject for Book 2.

57

Angels and Demons

There is a topic that I feel I must address even though it's controversial: Spencer's experiences with angels and demons. People may wonder, *if he doesn't speak, how would you know that he sees into the supernatural realm?*
As his mom, I just know. I believe he had visions when he was normal, but was too young to articulate what he saw. I believe he can see and hear things most people only dream about. Dreams they call nightmares or dreams from God. Signs and messages from God can often take on unexpected forms. Many do not speak of their experiences beyond what the natural eye can see, for fear of being labeled a freak, possessed by a demon, or mentally ill.

I have had visions myself but nothing close to the number of times Spencer has. I feel the presence of demons and angels, but have not seen them. Some might say this is a gift from God and maybe it's generational. It is not a *gift* one might ask for, nevertheless, it is part of Spencer's everyday life.

I have learned in my research that people who practice magic are different from those who see into the supernatural realm of God. The Bible speaks about donning the armor of God in Ephesians. For Spencer and our family, it was more than just metaphors. I tried to pray the armor over each individual, daily. The helmet of salvation, breast plate of righteousness, sword of the spirit, belt of truth, and feet prepared to walk the gospel. The armor kept the demons from breaking past the shields that our guardian angels set around us.

A glimpse of what Spencer experienced is only a guess, based on other stories of people who possess this gift. When I asked him if he saw his angels, there was always an eye to eye, soul connection that screamed, YES! When Spencer was seeing demons, I was praying them gone in the name of Jesus Christ. When he was seeing angels, a peace and presence of the Holy Spirit, light, and warm energy filled the room. These visions usually came during or after prayer time.

His visions or episodes are what the doctors called hallucinations. Many Christians believe that demons do not enter where the Holy Spirit lives. I disagree. I believe there is a fight from the moment you make that commitment to follow Jesus Christ.

When Spencer saw demons, his body manifested fear. He would breathe heavily, eyes focused in one spot on the ceiling or wall. His breathing would then turn into screams of terror. His body became stiff and literally shook with fright. Sometimes it was hard to decipher if it was a seizure or a vision. Screaming turned into crying. At the first sign of these episodes, I would be laying hands on him praying, calming, casting demons out of our space, in Jesus name. His heart would beat wildly and his eyes were like a deer in the headlights. My heart would break again thinking, *Lord, does he not have enough to deal with?* It did not seem like a gift at all.

There was one particular lengthy episode. Russ and I were entering our divorce phase. I stood over Spencer praying for 5-10 minutes. (Normally they dissipated in a couple minutes.) As I continued, my voice got louder, and my convictions were led by frustrations that however these demons got into our house, I was angry and they needed to go. I had done too much cleansing and praying over our property to be dealing with this! And why do they always pop in when you are utterly exhausted? Finally, I opened the front door and demanded they leave. I literally felt a whoosh of air rush past me. Spencer finally calmed down. This was not a practice my husband understood, nor one I particularly enjoyed. But it had to be done. Spencer lay in bed all night, eyes wide open, afraid to fall asleep.

Then there were nights when he would lie in bed all night, LAUGHING! Not kidding, hysterically laughing. We couldn't possibly get mad at him. Joy was a rare occurrence for Spencer, so no matter the time of day he expressed it, we embraced it. One particular night, we'd not slept well for several nights. I walked into suction Spencer's secretions from his uncontrollable laughter. He continued.

I said, "Dude, you have got to tell your angels to come back tomorrow. We need to sleep." He laughed harder. I picked him up and not so gently flipped him to his other side. "I will give you something to cry about in a minute, do you need a spanking?" I said jokingly. He laughed harder. By now Russ' curiosity got the best of him. He dragged himself out of bed and joined me. All we could do was laugh with him. After that he calmed down. Maybe he just needed someone to experience his joy WITH him. I've heard that there is no concept of time in the supernatural realm. This episode was proof.

Other times when he saw angels, as we put it, Spencer would start out by opening his eyes wide and they would begin to dart around the room. This is the only time his eyes would have this tracking ability and was my clue that angels had shown up. He would take a deep breath and short breaths would soon follow. Opposite of terror, an inexplicable excitement would come over him. His pupils would dilate and he would vocalize, as if trying to speak. There were so many times during these visions that Spencer was on the cusp of his first word. Usually during or following prayer, we would go into silent mode and watch in awe. If we tried to speak to him, he was unable to come out of his vision to make eye contact. He didn't want to. It was as if he was afraid to look away because he didn't want the experience to end. We'd revel in the peace of this supernatural miracle where we knew Spencer was getting messages about his life and purpose.

58

Evan

Evan's name means young warrior and noble protector. He is the introvert of the family; the quiet observer. He grew up to be an introspective, observant, and humble soul. The loss of his younger brother to brain damage set up an unwelcome chain reaction: the usual desire for adventure and the curiosity to learn had been abandoned, the awareness that your family is not whole and that your childhood is lost forever punishes you, frightens you. And what everyone sees when looking into you is that regret reached in and fished out the shiny, sparkling light in your eye. Emotion and commotion dampens your spirits until you are drenched by it and then you are left forever treading water trying to get afloat.

Evan felt a grave responsibility to care for his sister as well as Spencer, which caused him to man-up quickly and build some resentment in the process. He tried to accept all that he had been given, but it was a burden, too heavy at times. Often, when the house was empty, Evan would spend one-on-one time talking or reading to Spencer. Or sometimes he'd lie on Spencer's bed and watch TV with him. One of Spencer's favorite things to do was to sit by Evan while he played video games or talked with his friends. I think he felt like he was part of Evan's inner circle. I'd often walk by and see Spencer grinning from ear to ear or giggling about the teenage conversation in the room. Giggles usually came from a swear word or behavior defined as "unacceptable" by Mom and Dad. Evan helped out whenever asked; he mastered tube feedings, lifting, loading Spencer in the van, collecting and packing needed items and supplies. When Evan was in high school, he occasionally watched Spencer for an hour or so, when Nicole was gone and while I ran errands.

Through Spencer's ordeal, Evan learned not to take people for granted. He read the story of Helen Keller and learned that people with special needs can do some pretty amazing things if they can survive it, that is. Evan even learned to enjoy his dog more because he could no longer play with his brother. With nightly prayers, Evan's questions would rise to the surface creating a storm that I never saw coming. The silent currents that had been flowing underneath for years were rising as the waves of emotion needed to surface and be heard. Because Spencer's medical events happened just after the merry-go-round with Evan, he agonized over guilt as the perpetrator. He sunk into despair believing he didn't protect Spencer as much as he should have. I should have protected him better. I should have made him *keep his hands out of his mouth. I should have stopped him when he asked to ride the merry-go-round. We should have made him eat better* ... was the clutter locked in his head, wanting to be freed.

"Why didn't you stop it Mom? Couldn't you have stopped it?"

"Believe me, Honey, if I knew what I know now, I would have done everything I could to build up his immune system so that the virus would not have traveled to his brain," I assured him. "The virus was already in his brain— a combination of unusual circumstances that when put together caused something entirely different. No matter what, though, he was going to start having seizures anyway and there would have been nothing any of us could have done to prevent it!" Oh, if we could only go back in time if only to cross those t's and dot those i's JUST TO MAKE SURE.

Sifting through memories when they were an inseparable pair of brothers left Evan tortured knowing he and Spencer would never ride bikes together again, hike up the Castle Rock, sit on the peace rug, ski together, bonk heads on the trampoline, have late night talks about girls, or get into mischief around the neighborhood. All of those childhood events would be replaced with memories of a brother who sat in a wheelchair staring on as a silent observer. We discussed that it was okay for "Big Boys to Cry".

Evan developed a solid moral character early on, seeking friendships without bias regarding status, money, or accomplishments. He looked into people to determine their heart to make his connections with others. In third grade, Evan shared a poem his teacher gave the students—a beautiful illustration of how he lives his life. Step by step, day by day, steadily moving toward where his heart leads.

A candle is a simple thing; it starts with just a bit of string.

Yet dipped and dipped with a patient hand, it gathers wax upon the strand.

Until complete and shining bright, it gives at last a lovely light.

Our lives are like that string; each deed we do a simple thing.

Yet day by day if on life's strand, we work with patient heart and hand,

It gathers joy, makes dark days bright, and gives at last a lovely light.

I love you Mom and Dad!

Love, Evan

Evan eventually got reinvested in school, dirt biking, scouts, and belonged to a youth group. He aligned himself with his dad during all their scouting events and they have many fond memories together. Evan and I participated in a number of youth group events on Wednesday nights and weekends. We bonded during this time and I noticed that Evan became a deeply spiritual guy who seeks out answers to life's hardest questions. He worked through the difficulties and did well. He focused an artistic mind into making a bench out of an old snowboard. In fact, it was not uncommon to find Evan up in his room drawing or in the garage tinkering. After he got his driver's license, he'd head off to higher elevations for snowboarding, taking in the great outdoors, and his love of travel.

59

Elle

As a young girl, Elle would often sit next to Spencer in bed, reading to him. When she was three she made up the words, and it was adorable. Spencer LOVED it! She spent hours doing therapy with Spencer and our volunteers, and was my nurs-ing assistant whenever necessary. She was Spencer's cheerleader and could get him to do an exercise when all other attempts failed.

One day shortly after Spencer came home from the hospital, a three-year-old Elle walked up to me and said, "Mom Spencer is agitated. He needs his Artane." (the drug for Spencer's movement disorder.)

Looking at the clock I laughed. "You're right Missy." As a toddler barely able to talk, Elle reminded me that much of caring for a patient is in observing their behaviors.

Elle—meaning bright light—was just that in our lives. Her optimism and zest for life was a beacon on dark days. Her daring and adventurous spirit got her into some situations with broken bones and a rattle snake bite, but she serves you a story that will make you laugh every day. Her love for animals continues on. From bottle feeding two-week-old kittens when their mother ran away, to sneaking in a garter snake and putting it in an aquarium under her bed, to shoving a misbehaving kitty into a backpack and zipping it up. There was never a dull moment with Elle. She still blames me for running over our resident praying mantis that lived in our tree. She gave DC, the cat, a talking to for killing a toad that lived on our property for years. Caring for and riding horses together is our thing—relaxing, peaceful, and a form of therapy that we both craved. Interning two years at the Cheyenne Mountain Zoo encouraged her to minor in Zoology, and her passion for horses has led her to an Equine Sciences major. That girl goes after what she wants and this soul on fire is on an exciting journey!

Below is a commemorative speech that Elle gave recently about her life with Spencer.

Ordinary is a Relative Term

I come from an ordinary family, from an ordinary town, from an ordinary school, from an ordinary life. I grew up with two brothers, went to school, rode horses, hung out with friends, played sports, traveled—all the normal things that families do. As a child nothing ever seemed different, but I soon realized that not everything about my family was normal. My brother Spencer—a normal, healthy, active, ornery boy was diagnosed with viral encephalitis when he was six years old, and because I was only three at the time I did not know what had happened. His condition is an extremely rare brain injury caused by an unknown virus that travels up the spinal cord and into the brain, attacking the body. By the time he came out of the hospital he had lost almost all of his functions. He could not walk and was in a wheelchair, could not eat so was on tube feedings, could not speak, had a seizure disorder, and had lost over a quarter of his body weight. My family's life had dramatically changed, and while we tried hopelessly for years to re-establish his lost abilities with therapy, extreme medical treatments, countless trips to hospitals, a neurology conference in Norway, it was time to accept his condition and continue on with life. Spencer is now 22 years old and is still this way, but one of the most loved boys in my life.

Now... I have told this story over 400 times. Who knows how many. I have lost count. Trust me, that's the short version. Every single time I see the listener's face drop with sadness and pity, it is important to know that this is completely normal for me. I grew up with suction machines, wheelchair ramps, nurses, volunteers, and my world practically revolving around my brother, but my family still accomplished everything of a normal family. That to me is a miracle!

So why would I think any different since that was all I knew? Ask most people and they would agree with you that the situation is heartbreaking. We, in a way, lost a brother and a son to an unknown illness that randomly wandered into the middle of our lives. But after years of feeling angry, sad, and annoyed with our situation, I am now able to see how much I have really gained.

While it is very easy to be ticked off at the world, one thing that we must always remember is, it could always be worse. About a year after my brother's brain injury, he received a Make a Wish and we traveled to Disney World. As you can imagine, this was almost as stressful as fun for the entire family. I mean, you try flying on a plane with a hyper sensitive handicapped boy, a pair of excited yet arguing siblings, and of course an extremely stressed and annoyed set of parents. And we did so with over 50 other terminally ill kids who had also received a wish. We were surrounded with families going through the exact same thing, and unfortunately, not all as lucky. While we were there, one of our new friends died unexpectedly, never having the chance to complete her wish. This tragedy left us grateful for our brother. While Spencer is severe, he is stable. But one thing that trip taught me, was that even in the darkest of times, there is happiness in the world.

Not only has Spencer made me into one of the most positive, open, and talkative people, he has also prepared me for life. As we know, life has a tendency to slap us in the face at the worst times. It can be about as fun as running a 10k while trying to juggle chainsaws. Growing up with a medically fragile sibling can prepare for some of the chaos. I learned emergency protocol, nursing care, and of course how to stay calm in high stress situations; which turns out, is much needed when one is as clumsy as I am. I have broken several bones, and been bitten by a rattlesnake, and stung by a box jellyfish. My "frantic", is a frozen bag of peas on a rattlesnake bite, silent tears, waiting patiently for my mom to arrive to rush me to the ER. Then calming HER down in the car while asking her to call the ranch hand. I want that rattle!

Spencer has also had a big impact on everyone in our community. While he may seem powerless, he is MIGHTY within. He was featured on the Today Show in 2010, honored at our church and school, and has a book written just for him. Also as one of many forms of his therapy, Spencer started hippo therapy and as a three-year-old I tagged along and immediately became obsessed with horses. I would never be where I am today without him sitting at my shows and riding alongside of me. Spencer's life is a marathon and while excruciating at the time, he's been one of the most inspiring people in my life. As one of the most positive and courageous people I know, he can easily make anyone smile. Spencer also introduced me to one of the most loving communities in the world. Special needs individuals are among the most caring and optimistic people around. If you really take the time to get to know them, they can teach you so much. Getting involved with the Wellsprings community in my hometown and Spencer's high school class taught me how we see people differently. It taught me that being DIFFERENT is nothing to be afraid of.

At first glance it may seem that Spencer's life was ruined by this monster of an illness, but his joy, optimism, and warrior spirit have proven time and time again that life is precious and full of light and love. And at first glance, if one thinks he has nothing to give (which he totally does) he has taught me to live an anything but an ORDINARY life.

60

Russ (in his own words)

After growing up with a disabled brother I was feeling very blessed to have three normal, healthy children. That all changed when Spencer got sick. My first response was to figure out how to make him better. After the first few years of trying so many things with very little result I began lowering my expectations. First I wanted him to be able to walk, talk and eat. Later I would have been happy with communication. Not knowing what he thinks and feels has always been the hardest thing for me. I finally came to the realization that Spencer was not going to improve and my focus became maintaining what we had. I just wanted him to be happy and not suffer. This meant minimizing his seizures, making sure he didn't get sick and always trying to find things that he would enjoy.

Many times I would wonder why God chose me to be Spencer's father. I felt I had paid my dues growing up with my brother Will. His cerebral palsy and seizures limited what we could do as a family. Now I had a son that was so much more severe than my brother. I didn't want my other two kids to suffer from the limitations that I grew up with so we always tried to give them as much of a normal life as we could. This meant that many times, vacations and activities were done with only one of their parents while the other stayed behind with Spencer. After time I realized that God had chosen the perfect person to be Spencer's father. I had a job that allowed me to take off whenever I needed and provided me with the finances to hire caregivers, pay for the best of care and provide for all of my family's financial needs. Growing up with my brother allowed me to understand what my other two kids were going through. I also understood how the system worked for the disabled. My background in medicine helped me to make the best decisions for Spencer's care as well as communicate his condition to family members, caregivers and friends. It's true that I was a good fit to be Spencer's father, but I wasn't always happy about it.

As Spencer stabilized, so did our care situation. We had progressed from having him sleeping restlessly on our floor when he first came home from the hospital, to finally achieving nearly full time nursing care and moving his room to the basement so both he and the nurses could have privacy and peace. This also afforded me some normal sleep after 15 years of constant night time suctioning, repositioning and attending to every cough, whine and sometimes scream. It was a big adjustment and I was always hearing phantom pump alarms and coughs. These sounds woke me so easily over the years and I would spring up to attend to Spencer's needs. Now someone else was caring for him more and more but I still had the lifelong responsibility of having him in my basement. I still had to coordinate schedules, attend appointments, order supplies and care for him when someone called in sick or quit. I started to wonder if this would be my role for the rest of my life, or at least the rest of Spencer's.

One day I was talking to a friend about her disabled brother and she told me about a new home that he had just moved into. That's when I learned about Bethesda Lutheran Communities. After hours of research, meetings, phone calls and visits we were able to get Spencer on a wait list for their intermediate care facility. The house that we visited is one of only two in the state of Colorado. They provide 24-hour nursing care in a residential environment to six residences that all had a high level of care needs. Spencer qualified for the funding and would be accepted if one of the other residents either improved or deteriorated beyond the scope of the care provided. We were told that most of the residents had been there for many years and it could be many more before a spot could open up for Spencer. But it was a glimmer of hope that there could be a better life for us and for Spencer. To our surprise only a few months later we got the call that a spot had opened up. One of the residents had gotten ill and after a long hospital stay was going to have to move to a long-term care facility. In a matter of a couple of weeks Spencer was moving into his new home. It would be a trial period to see how he adjusted and if the staff could care for his needs. Spencer was going to be the most severe of the residents. In the mean time we needed to let our nurses and caregivers know about the move. We didn't want to lose anyone in case his new home didn't work out but didn't have much choice.

It's been nearly two years since Spencer "went off to college" as one of my friends says. It's been such a life changer for Spencer and all of us. The consistency of care at the home and the companionship of the other residents have allowed Spencer to be happy and healthy. His frequency of seizures has decreased and he receives continual therapy and stimulation at his day program. For his family, we finally get to be family members instead of caregivers. Our visits consist of stories, kisses and laughter. For me the burden of care has been lifted and I'm loving just being a Dad.

61

Angie

Spencer,

I wrote this poem when I was longing for the boy I once knew...before the virus, before neurological decline, before brain damage. This longing usually surfaces around your birthday or holidays.

Spencer, I know you have thought processes, but I am unsure about the degree to which you can think. I know you have feelings, but I cannot know what you feel. I know you have memories, but are they good or mostly traumatic? I'm certain you feel pain, but how often and on what scale? I want to crawl into your head and understand how your mind works. And when I can't, I write, I pray, and I talk to my voiceless boy. I get out my journals and I watch videos of you. I continue to read your eyes, I listen to your laughs and cries, and I hope for the day when you can utter a word. Just one word. That would be glorious!

God's Special Child

Refrain:
God's special child, like no one else,
The world sees your brokenness,
But to the Lord, you are whole,
He sees your heart, your spirit, your soul.

Spencer Lee please talk to me,
I want to gaze into your mind and see,
The words longing to be set free.
I need for you to speak your love for me.
Refrain.

Spencer Lee please walk with me.
Lord, release his legs to victory.
You are an inspiration, a saint to me.
I pray a glorious miracle for thee.
Refrain.

Spencer Lee come sit with me.
Let's talk, eat, laugh, and tease.
Reminiscing of how life used to be.
Now run along and climb that tree.
Refrain.

Spencer Lee come live life with me.
Live out the thoughts inside your head.
Experience the life that was meant for thee,
With God our Father through eternity.

I could go on and on in this chapter about so many "aha" moments in my walk with God and chasing healing conferences for that miraculous moment when my son would be whole again. I poured myself into self-help books, stories of near death experiences, and lots of programs and books on alternative medicine and health. With 169 hours in a week, if I wasn't caring for Spencer when Nicole was off, I was researching, journaling, or digging deep into my subconscious, my past, or genealogy to somehow find answers to my present. When I got frustrated with Spencer's condition, I refocused my attention on my husband, other children, or my passions.

My years of "acceptance" trying desperately to define a new status quo, were spent building a relationship with God that would carry me through each day. I moved beyond my Catholic roots to attend a non-denominational Christian church. I grew in my spirituality more in four years than I had my whole life. Our life situation demanded it. From 2003 to 2007, I intensely poured myself into conversations with God and searched for answers to life's difficult questions. Often times God whispered to me much like Spencer did, in my mind and my heart. He spoke through people, music, dance, travel, and nature. Water, whether it be a fresh shower in the morning, sitting at my favorite spot at the lake or on the shores of the ocean...water refreshed my soul and brought new revelation. When God seemed to be silent, I would try to rid my heart of all the anger, hurt, and un-forgiveness to allow love and light to fill the dark places again. God's WORD always brought me closer to HIS heart. One of my favorite quotes is: *Forgiveness doesn't excuse their behavior. Forgiveness prevents their behavior from destroying your heart.*

At the church where I felt our family was led, I had finally found my safe place, where I was accepted without conditions or works. I was saved by GRACE alone and that was a concept I had to learn over and over again. Living in a conditional world, I have to be reminded day by day, that no matter what I do, God still loves me unconditionally. My new church family taught me so much about LOVE and GRACE and it was a safe place for our family and the healing blanket to my soul.

Through much praying and processing, I realized that God did not want this to happen to Spencer. This is where God gets blamed much of the time, and as a result many depart from their belief in the anger stage of grief. One day I reasoned that part of living in an imperfect world is being exposed to illness. Spencer got sick and brain damage was the result—a process that would be viewed as natural selection by many. Where I blamed myself was in not knowing enough about boosting his immune system so the virus would not have traveled through the blood brain barrier—a mistake I would have to forgive myself for and let go.

To gain some balance and contribute to our community, I threw myself into youth ministry, classroom parent, facilitator of a support group for special needs parents, and dance class. I love my dance girls and still have a strong bond with the group we call "the sistas five". Tink, Pink, Lilo, Stitch, and Snap have come through a lot together and supported each other along the way. It is so important to have a group of peers that you can have fun with, but also be REAL with.

The extracurricular activities of HIPPO therapy (Spencer), Riding lessons (Elle), and motocross and Boy Scouts (Evan), pilot for Angel Flight (Russ) kept us busy beyond school. Russ and I claimed Thursday our day and strictly had a date once a week. Our rule was to talk about family business for 30 minutes, then move onto US for the rest of the evening. Our weekend trips away gave Russ and I the opportunity to revert back to our younger years and play. Family meetings kept communication open and honest, but they were not a favorite for anyone.

We would all heal together, support one another's passions and maintain what needed to be done for Spencer. It was a challenge, but we were determined to make it work. We learned to live by the motto:

Life is short, Live it!
Love is rare, Grab it.
Anger is bad, let go of it.
Fear is a mind killer, face it.
Memories are sweet, Cherish them.

The teens from church taught me more about life than all my years combined. Their unapologetic relationships with our Creator were humbling. One evening as I poured my heart out to God, God poured his heart into me and my first song was written.

RAIN DOWN- Spring 2003

Turn my sea of sorrow, into a sapphire sea,
Turn my mountain of fear, to Your majesty.
Turn my heart of anguish, to a gem for all to see.
Into a loving heart, that's been set free.

Refrain
Rain down, your love, Oh Lord
Rain down on me, Rain down
Rain down your love Oh Lord
Rain down on me. Rain down.

After the rain, would you bring the sun out again?
Fill my heart, with your love that has no end.
Touch the deepest part of my soul, oh would you mend.

I'll follow for eternity, wherever you send.

Refrain

Dance is a way I process my emotions and worship the Lord. In 2009 I was asked to dance at a women's retreat. I first gave my testimony and then expressed my love for Spencer through dance. The choreography and lyrics to the song "If You Want Me To" by Ginny Owens, comes to mind when I don't understand the ways of God. Ginny Owens is a contemporary Christian artist who is blind. Based on her music, it is comforting to know that she has also questioned the ways of God.

"Life is not about waiting for the storm to pass, it's learning how to dance in the rain."

Vivian Greene

62

Everyone Has a Story

April, 2010

Somewhere my phone is ringing . . .*Where's my dang phone...*"Hello?"

"Hello, Angela?"

"Yes. This is Angie."

"Hi, Angie. This is Kate Cook from the Today Show."

"Ummm, You might have the wrong number, how can I help you?" I said with a wrinkled brow.

"Your caregiver, Nicole has written a letter to us on behalf of your son, Spencer. We are considering her story for our segment called, *Everyone Has a Story*. Do you have time right now for me to ask you a few questions?" she asked.

Surprised, I said, "Sure."

The conversation lasted about fifteen minutes and I walked into my CNA class late. It was a lost day of instruction, as my mind was replaying the phone conversation. Nicole had not mentioned anything about this. When I arrived home for dinner, Russ and Nicole told me that Kate had a phone interview with both of them too. Kate needed a short video and a photographic timeline of Spencer from his normal years up to the present and it had to be in the mail by Monday. *Yes, I would do this, certainly.* If it changed one life, it would be worth the effort.

The Today Show collected the videos and pictures from three families for a contest on the *Everyone Has a Story* segment. The runners up were asked to watch the show because the winner would have to accept their invitation on live TV.

Nicole's story won! The story was selected on Monday, so all four of us (Nicole, Russ, me and Spencer) had one day to leave for New York by Tuesday so that our segment would air on Thursday. It was a whirlwind of activity: making arrangements for Evan's and Elle's sleepovers, notifying their school about their absence, canceling Spencer's many therapies. And, oh! I almost forgot! I had to find clothes appropriate for national television! I should be excited about an all-expense paid trip to a city I have never seen, but honestly, my main concern was getting Spencer there and ready for a TV appearance only one day after a full day of travel. And then it occurred to me that Spencer might vomit or have a seizure on national television! *Oh please Lord,*

I know these are common occurrences when Spencer is nervous and over stimulated. Please, please, please . . . and you know the rest.

From home to our hotel room, it was 12 hours travel time. Our plane circled LaGuardia for over an hour due to approaching thunderstorms. Spencer and I went to bed while Nicole and Russ headed to Times Square since it was within walking distance. They passed the Rockefeller Center, The Tonight Show, Broadway Shows, shopping, great restaurants, and everything else you could imagine. Kate arranged for Nicole and me to see *The Million Dollar Quartet*. She thrilled us with last minute front row center seats and *Elvis* threw me his scarf! So fun! Thank-you Kate!

We bedded down early on Wednesday evening. It was a restless night because Spencer was on a roll away bed next to us. Between suctioning and turning Spencer over every three hours, Russ and I were having Today Show nightmares. I was also coming down with a cold and hoped the camera would bypass me and stay on Nicole and Spencer. Hopefully Nicole would be fresh for the show. She had some peace and quiet and a suite all to herself. Spencer's shower without a handicapped shower chair was a challenge but we were all dressed and ready to go by 8 a.m. Kate walked over from her office to collect us.

Walking through the studio and watching the scurry of many busy people, reality set in. I hadn't been nervous up to this point; preparations and travel kept us and our thoughts occupied. We waited in the green room for them to call us for hair and makeup. Spencer slept. I sat next to him and gently rubbed his head to try to arouse him. Russ suggested that I DO NOT stimulate Spencer. Fear of a seizure was also on his mind.

We were prepped with a few questions that Kathie Lee and Hoda may ask and gave us brief instruction of what would happen once we were on the air.

Minutes before showtime, Kate came in and asked us if we had any questions. It was a 10-minute segment. *Shouldn't be too difficult, right? Please God, no vomiting, no seizure. Thank-you!*

Entering the studio, we passed another room where an NFL player was waiting with his wife. They would be talking about their special needs son right after our segment.

A booming voice filled the air. Hoda announced: "It's time to meet our newest *Everyone Has a Story* contest winner."

Kathie Lee: Nicole, A Colorado Caregiver wrote in to tell us about a very special young man who at just 15 years old is *her* inspiration. His name is Spencer McCombs and this is Nicole's letter.

"I write to tell you about a boy I think you should know. The boy who plays an integral part in my life is Spencer McCombs. Spencer is a fifteen-year-old who has inspired me to run the 2009 Chicago Marathon. Healthy until age 6, Spencer contracted a virus that ravaged his brain and left him severely affected. No longer able to walk, talk, or even eat on his own, Spencer's daily life is a marathon in itself. Completely dependent upon others' care for him, confined to his wheelchair, his frequent seizures all reflect the daily challenges Spencer must face.

"Along with *these* struggles, in the eyes of the world Spencer is in a sense a "nobody" that has nothing to offer. Well, I write on behalf of Spencer and for all who love him. This amazing boy, who appears powerless, is mighty and powerful in the way he influences and affects people's lives. His eyes alone communicate his "Thank-you" and "I love you"; his spirit shines bright to those around him. As his caregiver, it's Spencer's humble dependence which inspired me to lace up my sneakers again and go another mile. I run because he can't run for himself. *Someday though—on the streets of glory—sweet boy.* Someday.

"Spencer is most often acknowledged for his *lack* of ability. I introduce him today as the boy who inspires me to live the life God has called me to with more faith, love, and courage. I'm his caregiver, but he's my teacher." Nicole

Hoda: Nicole and Spencer are here as well as Spencer's parents, Angela and Russ. Welcome to you all.

Nicole, Russ, Angela: Thank-you.

Kathie Lee: It is not easy to travel I'm sure.

I was afraid to comment as I didn't want the show to begin with my travel complaints. So I shook my head and smiled.

Hoda: Nicole, you are lit from the inside. Tell us how Spencer has inspired you to run the Chicago Marathon.

Nicole: As I said in my letter, in the eyes of the world Spencer is in a sense a *nobody.* They tend to see the things that Spencer is not able to do. But the Lord sees that his spirit is whole and he is a beautiful boy. I spend my days with Spencer living for God's glory, praying that one day he will be able to run again. Until then, I will run for him.

Kathie Lee and Hoda: He is a beautiful boy! Wake up Buddy. You need to hear your song.

Nicole: (Caresses Spencer's head) Wake up buddy. You're missing your TV debut. Yeah, he's jet lagged.

Kathie Lee: Not *everybody* wants to be in show business! We are going to take a commercial break, but when we come back we will get a very special performance courtesy of the wonderful Dillon Pomeraz.

Hoda: We are back with more of the *Everyone Has A Story* with Nicole and the young man who is her inspiration, Spencer McCombs with his mom and dad.

Kathie Lee: . . . And now it's time for the song that was written just for you, Spencer. Wake up buddy. (nervous laughter). It's called 'In The Eyes of the World' and the acclaimed performer Dillon Pomeraz is here to sing it for *you*.

In the Eyes of the World

In the eyes of the world, there are people who seem
To have all that the good life can give.
They're happy and healthy and can afford *any* dream.
They *really* know how to live.
But then there are those who have none of these things . . .
Who struggle each day to survive,
Facing challenges each moment brings.
And we wonder why they are alive.
They can't speak, so what can they tell us?
They can't move, so where can they go?
They can't sing, so you think they'd be bitter and jealous.
But there's something they know, we all need to know.
There are lessons that they're here to teach us.
They have every good reason to BE.
If we open our hearts and allow them to reach us,
They've got something to show us that we need to see.
If only we'd bother to look in their eyes,
There's wonder and gratitude there.
They tell us the truth that we're living our lives
In a place deep inside we share.
It's something that most of us often ignore
As we fight for possessions and fame.
There's only one thing that is worth living for,

And that one thing is LOVE…
Life has no other claim.
They can't speak but their eyes tell a story.
They can't move but their souls still smile.
They can't sing, but their hearts sing a song filled with glory
Of a life, for its own sake, that's rich and worthwhile.
Let us speak, so the world hears their story.
Let us run, with the joy they impart.
Let us sing of the goodness, the grace, and the glory;
Our birthright that lives deep inside every heart.
In the eyes of the world, they have nothing to give,
But in truth they're the ones who can teach *us* to live.
So let's open our eyes, not be blinded by pride,
To discover where love and true beauty can hide.

Kathie Lee Gifford and David Friedman

Hoda: We're back with *Everyone Has A Story* honoring a very special young man, her Spencer McCombs.

Kathie Lee: Dillon Pomeraz just performed "In the Eyes of the World" for Nicole and the McCombs Family. Also with us is the composer David Friedman.

Hoda: Angela and Russ, how did you like the song?

Angela: Oh, it was b-e-a-u-t-i-f-u-l. I am sure we will be listening to it more when we get home.

Hoda: Angela and Russ, I understand you have two other children. How have they coped with the challenges of having a special needs brother?

Angela: Yes, we have Elle who is 14 and Evan who is 19 and in college. We have made it through relying on prayer, family, and community support, and some counseling.

Kathie Lee: I think it's important for families to get counseling in a situation like this to try to make sense of it all.

Angela: Yes, for sure. We also have our weekly family meetings which the kids don't like very much.

Kathie Lee: Who likes family meetings? I don't blame them.

Hoda: Nicole, you are currently training to run the 2010 Chicago Marathon? Are you using Spencer as your training partner again?

Nicole: Yes, I put him in his stroller and we run around the neighborhood. It's a good workout pushing him.

Hoda: I'll bet! It's time now for our favorite part: We know that Spencer takes horseback riding lessons as a form of therapy—Hippotherapy—so we have set up a summer scholarship in Spencer's name to allow someone *else* who might not have the necessary insurance to receive lessons. Thank you Boots and Saddles Therapeutic Riding Center.

Angela: Yeah!

Hoda: And our friends at Sports Authority have generously donated a $500 gift card for Nicole, because we all know you need your running gear! (Hoda displays a gift basket of goodies as she hands it to Nicole.)

Kathie Lee: Congratulations! Happy Easter Spencer. God bless you buddy!

As we were finishing, I chatted with Kathie Lee about the difficulty of our life with Spencer. I told her of my impending book, no deadline. *Will she give it a quick read if I give her the request to use her name?* I whispered to myself. We left the Today Show and were in the taxi within the hour, headed back to Colorado. Our first TV debut, a wrap!

Two years later, while selling my jewelry at a local arts festival, a special needs man walked up to my table. He stared

at the photo of Spencer where I display his bio, telling of how he inspires me to create.

"I know that boy! His name is Spencer. Wasn't he on the Today Show?" he asked.

"Yes, yes...he was. Did you watch that episode?"

"Yes, I did. He is a handsome and brave boy."

"Thank-you!" I smiled

One life changed, I thought.

63

Parting Ways

2011-2012

Lord,

Be with our family as we transition into two separate households. Let your eternal light radiate throughout both homes, that these children may know your loving kindness. Please let them know that their parents love them deeply and this is not their fault. Lord, let Russ and I grow strong in your love and live our lives according to your will, not our own. I pray for all the children of divorce, that they have both their parents in their lives and never have a doubt that they are loved and cherished, and precious in Your sight.

Amen

By February, Russ and I were separated. I poured my hurts, hang ups, and habits out to God while Russ got things in order for a divorce. By May, I was preparing for a medical procedure and passed out, hitting my head in the bathroom. Russ took me to the ER and the emotional disconnect I felt made me realize, while I still had a glimmer of hope for reconciliation, Russ was done. Two days later we filed for divorce. By June, I was headed to my parent's house with a mental breakdown, and then fled back to Castle Rock to take care of Spencer. For two weeks my fragmented family went to Kauai on vacation, without mom. During that time Spencer had 13 seizures in two days. I hired an attorney, and began gathering papers for a potentially long drawn-out season of good-byes.

After 22 years of marriage, I realized that thousands spent on marriage counseling would not change our differences or fears. Both hearts had to be open to a miracle transformation that God would surely help us with if we surrendered our control. But Russ and I were growing in different directions and the relationship became toxic. "Hurt people, hurt people" was an expression that rang true through the whole divorce process.

Our counselor once said, "I have been a marriage counselor for 20 years and I have never seen any couple try as hard as you two did." Our marriage was surrendered under the weight of living in constant crisis. It seemed we were a good team when it came to our children, so I suspect that is why God put us together, initially, but the tumult won in the end. It took four years for me to accept the fact that this book would not end with Russ and I making it and taking our lessons learned into a ministry to help other families with special needs children.

Russ and I orchestrated a plan to switch the children between us every Sunday evening. Spencer handled the changeover like a trooper! He must have felt the release of a spring-loaded tension and was relieved to be in a place of peace, quiet, and harmony. His temperament was more peaceful, playful, happy, he slept better, was healthier, and had fewer seizures. I am not sure if he understood the concept of divorce, but he liked both his parents better APART. If mom was happy, Spencer was happy.

One day, after laughing hysterically about some teenage dance move that my daughter was teaching me, she said, "Mom, I don't think I have ever seen you laugh this hard. I am glad you are so happy." As I absorbed that comment, I heard Spencer giggling in his room. This moment made me realize that I had buried myself for a long time and it felt good to see Angie rising to the surface again. It was also a relief to see my kids learning a side of me they probably had rarely seen.

PART VI

GLASS SEAS
REFLECTING
MOON BEAMS

"Memories are like moonbeams
We do with them what we will."
Bobby Darin

64

New World

2012-2014

New beginnings are often concealed by painful endings. I moved from my apartment to a ranch style home directly across the highway from our country digs. The divorce took a little over a year from start to finish and what a year  it was! This beautiful new home did not compare to the one I raised our kids in, but from the moment I walked in, it felt like home. My back porch overlooked the 9th hole fairway and beyond that was the view of the Front Range of the Colorado Rockies. It was my safe haven and healing place for nearly three years.

Our newest Angel, Lisa, had been with us for almost two years and it was obvious that God brought us another saint. She not only took exceptional care of Spencer, bonding with him almost instantly, but she also weathered the divorce with the chaos of working in two separate households. My sister in law, Michele was also one of our caregivers and after listening to all our divorce drama, I am sure she found comfort in her evenings home with her whole family.

I was now embarking on a new world of work outside the home and as a newly single woman. I spent the summer taking classes to get my recertification in teaching and update my nursing assistant skills/certification. I was sure I was done with caregiving and teaching, but it was a good backup plan for steady employment. After being a stay-at-home mom for 20 years, I questioned who would hire a 48-year-old woman with re-created skills and one who also had a severe needs child that demanded 24/7 care. But these days I did not let fear control me. I immersed myself in the passions that made me feel alive. Dancing, making jewelry, writing, travel. I put down my own anchor! Milestones!

Song of Solomon: 5:16 His mouth is sweetness itself, he is altogether lovely. This is my lover, this is my friend. O daughters of Jerusalem.

I had not been dating for 25 years, so I learned quickly that it is nothing like it used to be.

There were no rules based on age, etiquette, or otherwise. If I wanted to attract the type of man I wanted in my life and my children's lives, it was clear that I should make a list of dating rules and abide by them as closely as I could. So I sat down on New Year's Eve to create my own rules that includes what was or could be negotiable and what was simply not negotiable in an acceptable mate. When I showed the list to my friend Karen, she raised a brow and said, "Your expectations may be a little high, Ang."

Well, I am not going to settle. I'd rather be alone than settle and be miserable," I said.

Karen looked at me with compassion. "I understand and believe me, I get it. I just don't know if you will find all of these qualities in ONE man."

One of my dating rules was if I knew it was not going to work out by the third date, I would let it go, walk away and not look back. For the next two years of my life as a single girl, I learned it didn't take that long to know, so why waste his or my time?

At this betwixt period in my life, I was on the brink of change and in July I had purchased my first home as a single mother. The fear I once had was dissipating with each bold step I took toward my future dreams and aspirations. One Saturday morning, I sat in my garage trying to sell the last bit of stuff that I could not fit into my smaller home. A familiar face from bygone days at Columbine High School walked into my garage sale! Brian Smith! He was a kind, loving man that I'd known 30 years prior. As unexpected as the visit was, it seemed that time stood still. I sat in my cutoffs and t-shirt and he looked my way with his charming dimples and charismatic personality.

Ummm....intriguing. We reminisced while flipping our way through yearbooks I found from a freshly packed box. Brian and I briefly shared all that life had given us since graduation, an unspoken fact that time had NOT stood still. Now we were wiser, more patient, and owned some character flaws that had been ironed out from the valleys of life. Our conversation flowed freely. Laughter and talk of adventure made us feel like we were 16 again.

The move to the new residence was not easy on Spencer. There was construction around the new place all summer long and he was not sleeping well. In the midst of the busyness of moving and adjusting, Brian and I cautiously went on a few dates. The conversation and laughter continued to flow and the adventure was just what I'd been looking for. Brian had a calming presence; he had a way of balancing me. If I was high strung, he leveled me out. If I was sinking into a low, he'd take me on an adventure. It was as if God was answering my prayer, "Lord bring me a kind and loving man that I adore and who gets me and the circumstances in my life. Who's going to take on a boy like Spencer? I mean really? I can barely handle him anymore. I am so burnt out."

On a drive home from Colorado Springs one day he turned to me and said, "Angie, I want you to know that there is nothing, I mean nothing, about Spencer that scares me."

So many times he would say exactly what I needed to hear, when I needed to hear it. It felt like we had a soul connection—a feeling I knew well by being Spencer's mother.

Before I got any more crazy about this guy, I had better find that list of things I would not negotiate versus things I could. At this point, I couldn't think of any desires Brian didn't meet. The next day I reached into the side pocket of my computer bag and voila...there were my lists! I almost did not want to read them because Brian and I were getting serious, fast. If he met my criteria, then would I have to or want to get married again? I so wasn't ready. Being around my former husband and his new wife to work things out concerning the kids, solidified the fact that I wasn't ready to take on new nuptials.

After I read the first ten lines, I set the paper down and walked away, teary eyed. It was almost as if I had written the list with Brian in mind. I wanted to call Karen right away, but instead I tapped out my findings in a BLOG post. I realized I wasn't supposed to find that list until this day. It was one of those "aha" moments I won't forget.

Looking at the top 11 non-negotiables on my list, I somehow knew that Brian was brought into my life at the perfect time. I could appreciate the qualities that would make us fast friends, which was the basis of a fulfilling, loving relationship. Life is anything but dull or mundane with BAS. There is never a day when Brian's humor does not bring a belly laugh or two. His honest, open communication and ability to share his emotions brings a smile to my face and a warmth to my heart. A kindred spirit when it comes to adventure, we have a box full of scribbles on little bits of paper. These unforgettable moments in life remind us of the bucket list we share and the spontaneity that helps us cross off items on a regular basis. I love that Brian Akrigg Smith is intentional about living and that he chose me to share life with.

Through the terrible pain of divorce, I yearned to be in partnership with someone who had that which can heal others and our families...together (with God's grace and intervention). The children have grown fond of Brian. He accepts us as we are, brings laughter into every day, and flips the daily grind into adventure. We are all growing through a journey that we were meant and blessed to share.

65

My Never Became God's Plan

October 2014

The art of life is a constant readjustment to our surroundings.
Kakuzo Okakaura

Spencer never seem to adjust well to my new place. Not only was he not sleeping well, but he was screaming his head off and on, all night long. Nothing I tried seemed to soothe him. Was I losing my touch? Or could he just feel my impatience and burnout? The walking dead, Spencer and I were approaching our third sleepless night. Somehow I had to be picture worthy by the next afternoon, as Elle wanted a mom-daughter shot in her portfolio of senior pictures.

Lying in bed next to Spencer and singing or rubbing his head usually calmed him, but now it seemed to increase his agitation. I had new neighbors upstairs and I was concerned that they were being awakened and getting as frustrated as we were.

After I got Spencer settled, I lay in bed staring at the ceiling and let the utter frustration stream down my face. The lyrics of *Say Something I'm Giving Up on You*, rolled through my mind and off of my tongue. *I'm sorry I couldn't get to you. Anywhere I would have followed you. Say something…* I wanted to release Spencer's care to someone else—I couldn't take it anymore—but I wasn't sure I could trust anyone. Each time Russ would bring up the group home idea, I would think about it and my guilt and fear would choke me. This reel would play over and over again.

"I'm not ready! Putting him in a group home would mean I am giving up on him."

Spencer had a routine endoscopy that caused stomach bleeding and a familiar night at Children's. Russ and his wife stayed from 7 p.m. to midnight and I relieved them and spent the night to cover round the clock care until he was sent home. They returned at 10 a.m. and stayed until Spencer was released later that afternoon. Russ and I stared across the table with shaded eyes during the doctor's meeting Friday morning. No words were necessary. We were tired and wondering how many more times we'd be doing this. I went home and slept for four hours and then psyched myself up for a concert that Brian's band was playing downtown. It was a birthday party of 14 friends, tickets purchased in advance. Despite the last 24 hours of drama, life went on as planned and I put on a happy face. *Too much practice*, I thought as I winked to the lifeless woman in the mirror.

On Monday, Russ received an email from the facility where Spencer was on the waitlist. There would be a position opening up in a month. Did we want to give it a try? But…I wasn't ready, or was I? I immediately made an appointment with my counselor. I explained my feelings. Dr. Holly not only validated my feelings but she gave me a perspective of hope.

"Ang, it's understandable why you would be scared. He is your severely affected child who is fragile. You and Russ have taken exceptional care of him 24/7 for 14 years. Most people would have never done what you two have. I think you would be surprised. Spencer is more ready than you think. In a normal set of circumstances, at his age he would be finding his way into the world as a young man. Maybe he is ready to be in his own place among peers. I'm sure you can see him as often as you would like and you would be able to focus more on quality time with him. Not his constant care, which you have told me is exhausting."

Dr. Holly had a kind way of bringing me back to the reality that God is in control. I'm not. After all, wasn't this what I prayed for less than a month before during those sleepless nights?

For the next week, I focused on those thoughts and began to see this arrangement in a new way; a good way. I prayed for strength, wisdom, and for God to put things into place easily if this was His plan. September 19th we were having a meeting with the staff of the group home. There were many arrangements that needed to be made and paperwork transfers to be done by October 6th. Just as we were discussing all of our wonderful nurses and how his caregiver, Lisa of four years would be the hardest to tell, Russ' phone vibrated. The text revealed that Lisa was in the ER with four blocked arteries, needing stents. She would not be working for a while. She became very attached to Spencer having a deep bond with him spiritually, emotionally, and knew him inside and out. Again, Russ and I made eye contact and knew this was a sign that God was giving us about the timing of the situation. Russ moved forward with the paperwork and I agreed to come to his house for the next two weeks to care for Spencer during the day so he could work.

I spent much of those two weeks snuggling with Spencer, talking to him, listening to music together, reading books, and crying in bed next to him. When his therapy people would show up, many who had been with him for 14 years, I would swallow hard and explain to them what was to happen on October 6th. It was a decision I had told them I would never make. Two weeks of emotional challenges left me exhausted by 2 p.m. every day. Not to mention, I was in the house where I raised my kids for 12 years, talking with my former spouse and his new wife. We had a lot to discuss about what we needed to get done so this transition could take place as smoothly as possible. Often I wonder how Spencer was feeling about the idea. I couldn't think about it too long or my anxiety would flare. I asked Russ if he'd told Spencer about our plan and he said he did. I couldn't tell him until three days before. He listened without reaction. I'm not sure he understood.

So the first week in October I did something I never thought I would do. Russ and I put Spencer in a group home. Looking back, I can see how everything fell into place. God orchestrated it from start to finish. A month before Spencer's position opened up, I had found myself in the hallway of my new condo at 3:30 a.m. pleading with God, "Take this cup from me Lord. It's been almost 15 years. I can't do this anymore. My whole body is tired and worn out. I cannot work during the day if I am not sleeping at night. I am too old for this!"

October 6th came and went and Spencer has been in his new home for a year and a half now. It is nothing short of a miracle how well he has done with the transition; another sign that God orchestrated this process. Though I still see

Spencer one to three times a week, the fact that he loves his new home has helped the whole family with the transition. It is more centrally located than our place in Castle Rock, so Spencer gets lots of visitors. His staff says, "Spencer is a popular guy!"

The house he lives in is a ranch style home in a residential neighborhood, housing six clients from 21 to 50 years of age. Each of them has their own set of special needs, but Spencer has the most significant needs. There are 2-5 fulltime staff on 24/7. It's obvious that Spencer loves his nurses and peers. He has developed a relationship with them just like he had all his years at home. He has had fewer seizures and less illness since he has been there and that's monumental as he is around 40 clients a day at day program. I'm amazed!

Presently we are working with the speech therapist to get a communication device activated by Spencer's eye gazes. It may be a long process, as his movements are not consistent. We have been reading the book *Ghost Boy* together. I am hoping this will spark his interest and encourage him to try harder. The book has so many painful similarities to our story. We can only read 1-2 chapters each time I visit. Sometimes the lull of my voice puts Spencer to sleep and other times he is hyper focused on the story sharing laughs and watching me cry.

Spencer has also helped me finish this book. I bore him with endless talk about the chapters I have left to write. I show him book cover designs and ask which one he likes best. Then there are questions like: "Shall I have a book launch party? Will you come to one of my book signings?"…on and on. I am excited to see how he will respond when I finally show him the first copy. And even more, to see how he reacts as I read it to him.

My conversations with my voiceless boy never cease to amaze me. While speaking with Spencer, though my questions are not answered nor my words responded to, the conversation comes through a spiritual connection, reading paralinguistic communication, and playing the guessing game. Much of what Spencer tells me comes through his eyes. Through his beautiful brown eyes, I have seen pain, surprise, anger, fear, confusion, frustration, terror, contentment, happiness, but most importantly love. I have never had to stare so blatantly into a person's soul over and over again, nor anyone into mine in hopes of some small message. Perhaps a clue into what part of his brain is working? What thoughts he may be having? Memories? The frustration of an unknown etiology of illness, no diagnosis nor prognosis haunts us day after day. But looking into his eyes has taught me to let go of the "why", move forward telling all the lessons learned from the best teacher I have ever known—Spencer.

WE WHO HAVE A VOICE,
MUST SPEAK FOR THE VOICELESS.

66

Random Thoughts and Lessons Learned

Grief never ends…but it changes its passage, not a place to stay. Grief is not a sign of weakness, nor a lack of faith… it is the price of love.

Unknown

You may see people week after week that are well put together but screaming for help on the inside. Or maybe you see people week after week who are broken on the outside, but lit from the  inside—so much so that it radiates from their presence, their soul. I have learned that just because a person looks good, doesn't mean they feel good on the inside. And just because a person's body does not function on the outside, doesn't mean that they're not whole on the inside, or don't have a mind that works.

Did you know that 80% of communication is non-verbal? The way a person stands, walks, dresses, displays expression and emotion—body language tells a lot about a person.

In Spencer's case, for 16 years now we have learned how to clue into a voiceless boy. Embrace a mind where pathways are unknown, care for a body that refuses to function, and decipher words from a voice that communicates through sounds, laughs, and cries. Too often significant needs people are ignored or overlooked because they can't or don't demand attention or understanding. People are afraid of what they don't know. We learned how to deal with the effects of brain damage in our Spencer. We loved him enough to give him a chance at the life he deserves.

Being Spencer's mother is difficult and has thrown me back and forth between darkness and light for years. A question that came up often was: *Why was I chosen by God to be Spencer's mother?* My friend's answer surprised me. It was different from the rest. *"Maybe Spencer chose you."* That certainly took the blame off of God on those especially difficult days.

Being Spencer's mother is my greatest gift and my greatest burden. I do not see my role as special and Spencer's role as handicapped. In fact, it was quite the opposite. The burden of grief and the difficulty accepting our circumstances became my handicap, and Spencer was the special one who taught us lessons we would have never learned otherwise.

One of my favorite pastors once said, "What is it you are weeping over? That is where you are called. Your dream has to do with your biggest challenge." Leif Hetland.

Many of our marriage problems were blamed on Spencer. I could not put this on him. Spencer did not choose to be different. If he could, he would gladly be "normal". However, since he is different, he deserves special understanding, patience, acceptance, and love. He is our child and it is our right and our duty to guide him in finding fulfillment in life. Russ and I did the best we could, and we made a good team.

Yet we couldn't deny the amount of stress we endured in providing 24/7 care for 14 years. In addition, we raised two normal children on years of disrupted sleep. Though we were blessed with the finances to manage our situation, the pervasive sadness took over. At times, I resented Spencer for what he demanded from me. At times, I resented Russ for what he demanded from me. At times, I was relieved for what Evan and Elle demanded from me. It was a reprieve from the daily emotional roller coaster. I gave all I had to be a good wife and mother. That was my childhood dream. Somewhere in the midst of it, I lost my passion.

Soon every expectation of my life, how my dreams would unfold, vanished. I would be a caregiver my whole life. How could I believe that everything happens for a good reason? I took on the role of victim for years. I saw the ashes, but wasn't sure how to turn them into beauty. My blind faith would leave that job up to God.

Our ability to travel brought temporary happiness and allowed us to make memories outside of Spencer's care. My respite while caring for Spencer was always spending time with God—in scripture, music, books, writing, nature, relationships with others. I saw that others got to experience daily joy, but mine was only moments at a time. I saw a difficult life, not one of comfort, or one of ease. I envied others. I laid it at the foot of the cross over and over, and God always provided temporary answers, opportunities for respite, and guidance for the days ahead.

We braved people's reactions in public because Spencer deserved his place in the world as much as anyone. Often times, when I hopped into an elevator somewhere in our small town, I inevitably got that question that rolled off so many people's tongues. They'd stare for a moment, recalling a memory. I could feel it coming. *Aren't you Spencer's mom?*

I'd respond, "Yes, and Elle's and Evan's as well."

They would smile and say, "How is Spencer?"

I wanted to be known as a professional and mother of normal children also.

In telling my story, so often people's advice to move from grief into joy eluded me. Their suggestions sounded so simple, logical, SO black and white. What they didn't know is that I possess a lot of grey areas. I am not a black and white person. When a tinge of frustration entered, I calmly explained, "Imagine your baby at 3 months, never developing beyond 3 months, being sick for 14 years. It put things into perspective for them as my analogy was always met with silence. But I had to move past the victim mentality or it would keep our whole family from their destiny. God eventually moved us beyond the why, to lessons learned from the valley. Pay it forward, was another one of our mottos.

Our family found joy away from the care of Spencer. Engaging in other people's normal gave us hope. But guilt usually found me and brought me running back. I believed in my vocation as wife and mother, so even when it would have been easier to go back to work, I chose to remain home. Now I would have to come to a knowing that even though I thought I was Spencer's BEST, most valuable caregiver, my exhaustion was saying otherwise.

It is May of 2016.

I am sitting in a beautiful house, surrounded by dogs, dog sitting. I am blessed to have four uninterrupted days to finish this book. Since October of 2014, (when Spencer entered the group home) these events have taken place:

- Elle graduated high school and finished her freshman year at CSU
- Spencer has four new best friends and five wonderful caregivers.
- Evan completed college and graduated from Western State University
- Russ has remarried and set up permanent residence in Costa Rica
- The house where we raised our kids is on the market
- I met my new love, Brian Smith
- I have worked five part-time jobs, still trying to figure out my dream vocation
- I purchased my first home as a single mom
- Traveled to numerous places
- The kids and Russ have done their traveling as well

Spencer's miraculous adjustment to his new home has released me to rediscover myself. The rest of the family has done more of the same. All of us are continuing to move toward our destinies, which Spencer has helped us discover. When you live with someone for years, who will never have an opportunity to realize their dreams, (this side of a miracle) it becomes a goal to move into passions of the heart, *every day*. To arise healthy and able is not a gift that we take lightly.

By getting in touch with our own souls, Savior, and surroundings we all learned ways to eliminate those lies that we are *not enough* or we do not *have enough* to succeed. Thank-you Kary Oberbrunner! It is an ongoing process, but Spencer's tragedy pushed us beyond our comfort zones to approach our fears. We refuse to let our past sabotage our future. The journey in achieving what God has placed in our hearts is transforming us into the people we want to become. Spencer also taught us to *never, never* give up. Most of the time, when people quit, they are closer to the goal than they think. Much of what each of us does is in honor of Spencer and the life he has suffered through. Living life with a significance needs child shakes a person to the core. It makes one dig deep to find answers to the meaning of life—theirs and yours.

Someone once told me, "Refuse to allow your life to be defined by loss and grief. Push through to new horizons and possibilities of what can be, rather than getting stuck in what has been. Your past does not define your future."

And so…each of us moves forward in our own way. We continue to heal, find happiness, and help others in need.

67

Full Moon

Cabo 2013

Are our conscious visions God's way of giving us hope for the future? Or are they just an image, a gift of beauty, or a sight to prompt a thought, an emotion?

On Good Friday, Elle and I walked out of our condo in Cabo to go to dinner. It was our first mother-daughter vacation since the divorce. In the sky, we saw a phenomenon neither of us had experienced before. It stopped us in our tracks. The full moon was low over the deep blue sapphire waves, and the light beams shot out in the perfect form of a cross. The wide beam of light covering the water teased us, looking like a golden road leading us straight into eternity. It took our breath away.

A friend once told me that this image of the moon happens only every 75 years. I am not sure this is true, but it felt like it.

We walked out to the rocks overlooking the ocean and embraced this gift from our Creator in our own way. I danced and she stared in a moment of silence. And then… we captured it on our phone cameras! We had no idea what this vision meant at the time. But we KNEW that it was a sign given to us for some reason.

As I lay in bed that evening, I remembered a dream that I had had several years before. The dream reminded me of the reason I love water—the ocean. Let go, let God was the message, and it allowed me to turn over the control that I never had in the first place. A life-long lesson that would humble me each time I released what wasn't mine.

It was an overcast day and I walked out to the beach. I saw two people sitting on the shore looking out over the ocean. Somehow I knew they were in a private conversation, and I did not want to disturb them. There was a certainty that these two people were MY people, but the distance made their names a mystery. Sitting from afar, the soothing sound of the waves and smell of the sea, brought peace. My eyes became heavy. Starting to doze, I saw in my periphery, MY people stood up and turned to one another, hugging. Then they began to walk toward me.

One of them was wearing a white robe with a green sash adorned with golden thread, a wreath of olive branches around his head. My heart beat wildly with excitement as I realized that my people were JESUS and SPENCER! I ran toward them and we embraced. I was overcome with JOY!

Then Jesus said, "Let's dance." I backed up six feet, curtsied, then bowed before Him. Jesus mirrored my bow. Jesus, Spencer, and I joined hands in a circle. We walked in, standing face to face. We lifted our joined hands waist high, palm to palm, then raised them to the sky, around and back down again. Jesus took turns dancing with me, then Spencer. The dance reminded me of a waltz or a contemporary form of worship. Jesus was a good leader and movement flowed freely. At the end of our dancing, we joined hands once again, Jesus in the middle. We walked toward the waves, my left hand outstretched, Spencer's right hand outstretched. As the water washed over our feet, we bowed.

Jesus released us and walked back twenty feet, turned around, stirring the wind, with his robe flowing, He stretched out His arms. We both ran to him for an embrace. He handed me a piece of white sheer fabric about 15 feet in length. He handed Spencer one like it that was blue. We ran in opposite directions, with the fabric over our heads, trailing like a kite. With the strong, steady wind, the fabric rippled beautifully behind us. Spencer and I ran back, making a circle around Jesus before we came back together. Jesus joined hands with us again, walked us to the edge of the water, and asked us to sit down. We lay down and let the waves wash over all three of us.

I am your living water. I run through you continuously. I am always with you. I am the roots to your tree of life. Without me, you will wither and die. With me, you will bear much fruit. When you have had enough of this world, take your mind to your artistic side, your passions. When it is not safe to indulge in your passions for fear of judgment, you can indulge in them with me. Today we danced. You are my beloved and I am yours. Angela and Spencer, I am well pleased with you.

Angela, when you are leaning into Spencer crying, I am embracing you, crying. As your tears fall on Spencer, my tears fall on your shoulder. When you are in his bed holding him, I am holding you. When you are crying out to the Father, I am too. When you cannot possibly think of one more prayer to say, I pray for you.

Spencer, the undercurrent of the ocean is constantly flowing, ever changing. On the surface we may see calm or a storm. Think of me working in your body like the currents

of the ocean. Though you cannot see, I am constantly doing a work in you. Above the water through the storms, I am healing. Through the calm, I am healing. You may not see the work I am doing, but it is ongoing.

I suffer with you. I will never leave you nor forsake you. You are my beloved and I am yours. Until we dance again. Jesus

Meanings of items in my dream:

Olive branches symbolize power, they betoken friendship and success

Salt water symbolizes tears of grief, tribulation and affliction

Water is referenced over 1,000 times in scripture and means refreshment, irrigation, and growth. Symbolically water is the word of the Lord, a stream or issue of spirituality, a body or collection of knowledge or teaching. Water represents the Holy Spirit.

Washing prophetically can be seen as a divine cleansing or baptism in preparation for induction into divine service.

Whirlwind represents divine power initiating action. The turning wheels of God.

White symbolizes triumph, victory in conflict, righteousness and purity, holiness and success.

Blue is a color that prophetically has celestial and heavenly power, spiritual dominance, unimpeded growth, unlimited potential. God's appearance.

Green means go, divine activity, linked to wealth and prosperity.

And so our lives continue to ebb and flow like the waves on the shore. The mysteries of life and incredible power that

the ocean holds in its depths still frighten and intrigue me.
But I know now that I can handle whatever comes and stand
strong in the current and still enjoy the water that swirls
around my feet.

faith hope love

Launched But Not Anchored

At early dawn the ship is launched on the calm ocean waves of life that continually break against the shore converting the stillness of the morn into a paradise of joy. The cool breeze wafts silently along on the wings of the summer air, causing the sails to flutter in the radiant sunshine. The vessel is ready to depart. Launch but not anchored. Where shall it anchor?

Like unto ships far off to sea. Outward or homeward bound are we.

Standing with reluctant feet, where the brook and river meet.

How close this Ship's changes resembles our lives. Its sunshine and tempest are our joys and our strife's.

We shall call Hope our guiding star.

Faith will be our compass which will lead us safely home.

The daisy as a symbol of love and innocence will be our ensign.

Reason our rudder.

Good conscience, its hinge.

Our stern is Freewill, but our main mast is the Banner of Truth.

Under the floating pennant of blue and gold we will float onward through the deep blue ocean under the golden skies.

Commencement address by my grandmother—
Helen Brown-Haag
1926

Notes

Chapter 1: Quotes by Michelle Hutton, goodreads.com
Marianne Williamson quotes

Chapter 2: Poem written by Angela Dee

Chapter 4: Top 10 Chilling Quotes During School Shootings, listverse.com

Chapter 9: Grand Mal Seizure, EEG, CAT scan, mayoclinic.org, m.kidshealth.org, healthline.com

Chapter 10: Epilepsy, uchealth.org

Chapter 16: Little Tin Soldier by Hans Christian Andersen
MRI, m.webmd.com

Chapter 20: Sacrament of Last Rights, wikepedia.org

Chapter 21: Hebrews 6:19 NIV

Chapter 22: Viral Encephalitis, Medscape.com

Chapter 25: Strep Throat, mayoclinic.org
Antibiotics damaging immune system, naturalhealth365.com

Chapter 27: Mother Teresa Quotes, mobilebrainyquotes.com

Chapter 28: NG tube, patient.info/health

Chapter 30: Atlas Man, wikepedia.org

Chapter 31: Holy Eucharist, ewtn.com

Chapter 32: Let Go and Let God, Proverbs 3:5 NIV

Chapter 33: Romans 5:3. NIV

Chapter 34: Jeremiah 31:25, The Message
1 Thesselonians 5:16, NIV

Chapter 36: IVIG Treatments, primaryimmune.org

Chapter 38: PICC Line and Broviac Catheter, pediatric-surgerymd.org

Chapter 40: Enterovirus, Herpes 1 and 2, CMV, Myco-plasm, Arbovirus, Varicella, EBV, Human Herpes Virus 6, Bacterial Viruses Brucella, Lyme Disease, Bartonella, Tuberculosis, RPR, VZV, Ab Reactive, St. Lois, Lacrosse Western Equine, Eastern Equine encephalitis, Asian Flu, Hepatitis, Myelin basic protein, Sillenium, Lead, Thallium levels, Syndenham's Chorea, SSPE
Wikepedia.org, mayoclinic.org, mosquito.org

Chapter 43: OT, PT, and Speech therapy, aota.org

Chapter 44: Bath Chair, maxiaids.com

Chapter 45: Prayer by Angela Dee
Daily List, p2p-co.org

Chapter 47: NACD, nacd.org

Chapter 49: HBOT, mayoclinic.org
Glutathione Treatment, m.webmd.com

Chapter 50: It takes a whole village..., afriprov.org

Tube Feeding Juice Recipe: Nutritionist from Denver Children's Hospital
    Meat/Vegetable
    3 Cups Fresh Vegetable Juice (Spinach, Cucumber, Carrot, and Celery)
    1 Cup Rice Cereal
    1 Cup Plain Yogurt
    ¼ Cup Olive Oil
    ¼ tsp. Iodized Salt
    1 Scoop Protein Powder
    3 Jars Meat Baby Food
    2 Cups Rice Milk
Blend altogether in Vitamix Blender for 3 minutes; put 12 ounces per seal a meal bag. Makes approximately 4-5 bags per recipe.

Chapter 51: GKTW, gktw.org
Make A Wish Foundation, wish.org

Chapter 52: Quote, readingemerson.com
HIPPO Therapy, americanhippotherapyassociation.org
Angel Flight Colorado, angelmedflight.com
Luke 22:39-46, NIV; 1Deuteronomy 31: 7-8, NIV

Chapter 53 & 54: Carrick Institute, carrickinstitute.com

Chapter 55: Poem by Nicole

Chapter 57: Angels and Demons,
eliefnet.com, bible-knowledge.com
Armor of God, Ephesians 6: 10-18, NIV

Chapter 58: Poem by Helen Custer, ypsigleanings.aadl.org

Chapter 59: Ordinary is a Relative Term by Elle McCombs

Chapter 60: Bethesda Lutheran Communities, bethesdalu-
therancommunities.org

Chapter 61: Poem and song by Angela Dee,
Ephesians 2:8, NIV,
Quote by Vivian Greene, goodreads.com

Chapter 62: Today Show-Everyone Has A Story, April 1,
2010 segment, Today.com
In the Eyes of the World Song by Kathie Lee Gifford and
David Friedman
Letter by Nicole

Chapter 63: Prayer by Angela Dee

Chapter 64: Song of Solomon 5:16, NIV

Chapter 66: Quote, inspirationonline.com
Kary Oberbrunner, karyoberbrunner.com

Chapter 67: Let Go and Let God, Proverbs 3:5, NIV,
biblereasons.com

Meaning of items in dream, The Prophetic Dictionary by
Paula A. Price, Ph.D., drpaulaprice.com

Acknowledgements

To my Creator, God. My source of life and strength, and the giver of love and all knowledge.

And the one who died for me, Jesus Christ—I give my utmost gratitude.

To my children Evan, Spencer, and Elleya—my young valiant souls of the next generation. Without you none of this would have come to fruition. I love you to the moon and back!

To my mom and dad Charlotte and Richard Swisher, my siblings Carmen, Blane, Brent, Brad, and Shawn. Without the love and strong support of family, I would not be who I am today.

To my family and friends, who stood by me and made sacrifices as I spent hours away from them to write.

To my proof readers and truth tellers, Chris McCullough and Barb Henderson—Thank you for cutting out all the rabbit trails.

To my editor and life-long friend, Tamara Trudeau—who would have ever thought we'd be here 42 years later? So blessed to have you in my life. A million hugs.

To my biggest fan and best friend, Brian Smith—You endured my hangry moments, sleepless nights, and emotional roller coasters. I love you!

To Kathie Lee, Hoda, and NBC Crew—Thank-you for choosing our story. If one life was changed, it was worth the trip to New York City!

To Kary Oberbrunner, my mentor and coach. I have been writing this book for 16 years and have wanted to be an author since childhood. It took your workable program, Author Academy Elite, and your belief in me to finally make my dream a reality. Thank-you!

About The Author

Angela Dee is an author, speaker, and teacher. A proud mother of three and a Denver suburbanite, she enjoys all the outdoor activities of Colorado with her family.

Angela's purpose is to encourage others who are facing life's hardships to find healing. Angela struggled to find her own clear voice and purpose beyond stay at home mom/ caregiver. Her life motto, *Be Brave, Dream Big* encourages others to live an anything but ordinary life! To never, never give up.

Angela's passions are creating jewelry, writing, and traveling. She is currently developing the content for her second book. She is a member of Igniting Souls Tribe and Author Academy Elite led by Kary Oberbrunner.

If this book has had an impact on you, Angela Dee would love to hear from you.

Authorangeladee@gmail.com

To contact Angela Dee for speaking engagements:

EMAIL
Authorangeladee@gmail.com

WEBSITE
angeladee.life

She may also be found on
Twitter: AngelaDianeMcC1
Instagram: angela.author
Facebook: Voiceless-Spencer's Story